Culturally-Conscious

WORSHIP

KATHY BLACK

Chalice Press®
St. Louis, Missouri

Bible quotations, unless otherwise noted, are from the *New Revised Standard Version Bible,* copyright 1989, Division of Christian Education of the National Council of the Churches of Christ in the United States of America. Used by permission. All rights reserved.

Cover art: Photos of fabric provided by Kathy Black
Cover design: Elizabeth Wright
Interior design: Wynn Younker
Art direction: Elizabeth Wright

This book is printed on acid-free, recycled paper.

Visit Chalice Press on the World Wide Web at
www.chalicepress.com

10 9 8 7 6 5 4 3 2 1   00 01 02 03

Library of Congress Cataloging–in–Publication Data

Black, Kathy, 1956-
    Culturally-conscious worship / Kathy Black.
        p.   cm.
Includes bibliographical references.
    ISBN 0-8272-0481-7
    1. Public worship.   2. Multiculturalism–Religious aspects–Christianity.
I. Title.
BV15. B57 2000
264–dc21   00-009776

Printed in the United States of America

Culturally-Conscious

WORSHIP

dedicated to
Taramin, Tanner, and Aubrey

Contents

Prelude

The question "How does/should one design worship in a multicultural context?" was asked several years ago by students and clergy in the Los Angeles basin. I was fascinated by the question since I had asked a similar question in 1980 when I was appointed as a chaplain at Gallaudet University (a college in Washington, D.C., for students who are deaf) and associate pastor of the Washington United Methodist Church of the Deaf. This was a cross-cultural appointment for me, and I learned much about pastoring in a community whose culture and language were different from my own.

From that experience, I knew that the question "How does/should one design worship in a multicultural context?" could not be answered until we knew at least the basics of how persons of other cultures worshiped in a more homogenous context. So I set out on what I considered to be a prerequisite research project, studying the worship practices of the twenty-one different ethnic cultures within The United Methodist Church. That resulted in the book *Worship Across Cultures* (Abingdon Press, 1998).

Talking with clergy and laity of these various cultures, worshiping in their congregations, and writing that book with twenty-five coeditors was not only a deep and rewarding experience for me, it was a crucial prelude to this book on culturally-conscious worship. The rich diversity of worship practice that I experienced around the country in these congregations has led me to believe that worship in multicultural or multiethnic contexts should be conscious of the "liturgical homelands"[1] of the cultures present in the congregation.

If you are pastoring a multicultural congregation and are in need of some of the basic issues and questions to ask surrounding a Korean funeral or a Filipino wedding or a Vietnamese baptism, *Worship Across Cultures* is the resource to consult, not this text. This book is about

---

[1] Carol Doran and Thomas H. Troeger, *Trouble at the Table: Gathering the Tribes for Worship* (Nashville: Abingdon Press, 1992), 23.

designing worship (primarily Sunday morning worship) on a weekly basis in multicultural congregations. It deals with the cultural conflicts that arise in regard to the various expectations people bring to worship and the cultural complexities that need to be faced to develop a shared story, a common memory, a new congregational culture in the midst of such tremendous diversity.

I am grateful for a sabbatical granted me by the Claremont School of Theology, a research grant from the Wabash Center for Teaching and Learning in Theological Education, and the students in the Multicultural Worship class who helped me hone the questions and issues this book addresses. I am most indebted to Dr. Mary Kraus for imagining the term *culturally-conscious worship* as a way of articulating what this book is about. Her marvelous hospitality also allowed me a place to write away from the daily distractions of my life in Claremont. She, along with my colleague in worship, Jack Coogan, were also helpful dialogue partners throughout the process.

Gratitude goes also to the many pastors I have talked with and the multicultural congregations I have visited for their hospitality in sharing their multicultural worship practices with me. It gave me a feel for the various models of worship that currently exist in multicultural contexts in this country. It is my hope that the models presented and the information found within will stir the imaginations of your minds and hearts to think intentionally and theologically about the design and content of worship in multicultural contexts.

Introduction:
Dreams, Definitions,
and Demographics

When I was beginning to write this book, I had a strange dream one night. In the dream, I was in a car driving to a lake when we passed a large field. The cars in front of me had slowed down, and some had pulled over to get a better view of what was in the field. As we approached, there in the middle of the field was the strangest creature I had ever seen. It had a body about the size of a cow, but the hair on the body was like that of a shaggy dog. The head and tail looked like a Brontosaurus dinosaur. Its neck was long and skinny and smooth and very flexible. The neck could be as short as the neck of a horse or extended as long as the neck of a giraffe. On the back part of the body were two horns that resembled the pointy nose of a rhinoceros. Clearly these horns were prickly at best and possibly dangerous, but we were not afraid of the creature. Everyone in the car kept asking, "What is it? What is it?" "I don't know," I replied, "but it sure is fascinating! Let's find out."

That's exactly the question I ask when trying to describe the creature some call "Multicultural Worship" and I have come to call (with the help of a friend)[1] "Culturally-Conscious Worship." What

---

[1]Many thanks to Rev. Dr. Mary Kraus for imagining this term, *Culturally-Conscious Worship,* to define what this book is about.

is it? It's a strange-looking creature, but it has familiar features. It reminds us of an ancient past but is clearly something new. Parts of it are inviting, like a big shaggy dog, but parts of it are scary, and we're not sure how close we want to get to it. It is mysterious and beyond our reach, yet exciting, calling us to further investigation. Some look at it from the safety of their cars, and others want to see it up close, to get involved with it.

But what is multicultural worship? On the one hand, it can be argued that all worship is multicultural. In a homogenous African American service, there are elements from various parts of Africa that were brought by the people who were taken as slaves to this country. These rituals and practices were merged with the white missionary teachings of their masters, along with their own liturgical creations on this soil, the spirituals.

The liturgy of a congregation that is entirely composed of European Americans is likewise multicultural in its history. We sing hymns from German composers and British composers and American composers, both black and white. Our eucharistic prayers come from Paul and the early church in the Mediterranean area, including North Africa. Other prayers come from various parts of Europe and the United States.

And yet, within any denomination, people struggle to hold on to their "traditional" worship practices as if they were stagnant entities for hundreds of years. Introducing change in a worship service is often met with, "We've never done it that way before." And yet the reality is that worship has been in flux since the beginning of our history.

Throughout history, most worship services have been "multicultural" to some degree in that they contain elements from diverse cultures, including roots in Jewish worship. Few, if any, liturgies derive their material from a single culture. However, claiming that all worship is multicultural in its very nature masks the real differences that congregations are facing today when persons of very diverse cultures worship together. The past thirty to forty years have had a major effect on the cultural makeup of many congregations in urban, suburban, and even rural areas. Many multicultural congregations are struggling today with what it means to worship in such a diverse context.

The assimilationist policies of the United States forced early immigrants from various parts of Europe to give up their native languages and cultural practices and join the "melting pot" of American culture. To a large extent, this worked because in their physical appearance, the people looked enough alike that once they gave up their native languages (other than English), these Europeans could blend into the "look" of being American. But the early immigrants from China and Japan did not have the same choice, since their facial features did not allow them to "blend in" in the same way.

Since the 1960s and 1970s, however, many persons who belong to cultural and linguistic minority groups are trying to reclaim or maintain their ethnic histories, languages, and cultural practices. The "melting pot" image has been replaced with the "salad bowl" image, where we are all in the same bowl, but our uniqueness is clearly visible.

In addition to the movements happening within this country, there has also been a recent influx of immigrants to this country as a result of various wars and upheavals in other lands. The Korean War, the Vietnam War, the war in Cambodia, the war in Nicaragua, the upheavals in China and Cuba and Haiti are just a few. These migrations of people from all over the globe have had a major effect on our increasingly multicultural society. The more recent immigrants bring with them their belief systems, worldviews, cultural values, and ritual practices—including worship.

Many Christian immigrants seek out a congregation composed of persons from their native culture or persons who share their native language. Having worship in their native language and in the style and form that are familiar to them provides a touchstone for them in this foreign land. For many communities, this time of segregation is important for both spiritual and cultural enrichment. It is in homogenous worshiping communities that the rich language(s) of their native land is spoken, where the music is in the rhythm that beats in their bones and where the prayers that express their deepest struggles and most intense joys are offered.

In these more homogenous congregations, God is praised in Cantonese or Spanish, Korean or Fanti, Tagalog or Creole, Vietnamese or Samoan, Lao or English. Singing may be accompanied by guitars and maracas, or piano and organ, or African drums or Native American drums or Latin American drums—each with their own distinct shape and sound, but all beating the heartbeat of the world. Some sit quietly in sincere reverence while others dance for joy over what God has done in their lives.[2]

---

[2]Kathy Black, *Worship Across Cultures* (Nashville: Abingdon Press, 1998).

Those who have immigrated to this country bring their "liturgical homelands"[3] with them. They bring the sights and sounds and touches expressed in their worship traditions, the ebb and flow of celebration and meditation, the depth of their belief and their commitment to God. In times of transition and turmoil (which many immigrants experience in this country), their "liturgical homelands," a sense of cultural familiarity as well as a faith community, are crucial for planting one's feet in new soil and not only surviving but growing–supported by the community.

So while this book is about worship in multicultural congregations, I want to recognize the importance of homogenous faith communities, especially for new immigrants. For many, the survival of their language and culture in future generations is dependent on a strong ethnic congregation.

Multicultural Church but Separate Worship

One model of the multicultural church that can be found in several cities around the country is a congregation with two or more worshiping congregations organizationally structured under one multicultural church. Each subgroup worships in its native language. So a congregation may have three pastors on staff: one for the English-language ministry, one for the Korean-language ministry, and one for the Spanish-language ministry. While the administrative tasks, outreach ministry, and other programs of the church are done collectively, worship (and other activities such as religious education and fellowship times) may be conducted in their respective languages. The entire congregation comes together a few times a year for a common multicultural worship service, but for most Sundays, none of the three worship services conducted are multicultural. This model not only allows for a multicultural context, a greater pool of resources, and shared facilities, but it also honors the language preferences and unique worship styles of the various cultural communities represented in the congregation.

Multicultural Church with Multicultural Worship

Despite the number of persons who join ethnic congregations or who join multicultural congregations with various language ministries that hold separate worship services, there is still an increasing number of congregations in this country that are composed of persons of

---

[3]Carol Doran and Thomas H. Troeger, *Trouble at the Table: Gathering the Tribes for Worship* (Nashville: Abingdon Press, 1992), 23.

different races, ethnicities, and cultures. Many of these worship services are conducted in the English language. For many recent immigrants to this country, one of the first goals is to learn the English language. Attending an English-speaking church and developing supportive friends in the congregation who are native English speakers are steps in achieving that goal.

Other congregations are composed of persons from the Philippines or from Africa, where there are so many languages spoken among the islands (Tagalog, Ilocano, Pampango, etc.) or among the various countries and tribes of Africa that English is the language most have in common. But multicultural worship services are not limited to English-language congregations. There are multicultural worship services conducted in Spanish or conducted bilingually in a Chinese congregation in Cantonese and Putonghua (Mandarin) or conducted in French and Creole in a Haitian church.

A historic European American congregation now has a large Filipino population comprising more than a third of its membership. A large European American congregation in a city that is predominantly black has just called an African American to be their senior pastor. A congregation whose charter members were from Mexico is now composed of persons from Cuba, Argentina, Guatemala, Puerto Rico, El Salvador, and Ecuador. A traditional African American congregation now has members from various countries in Africa and the Caribbean.

The membership of a European American church has been rapidly declining over the last decade. A church in Los Angelas had a choice of closing or inviting another congregation to merge with them and assume primary responsibility for the facilities. They offered it to a Native American congregation, and the remaining remnant of the European American congregation joined the Native American church. A Japanese church composed of second- and third-generation Japanese conduct their services in English. Over the past few years more and more one and one half generation (moved to the United States as children and were educated here) and second-generation Koreans and Chinese have joined this church, making it a pan-Asian congregation with Japanese clergy. The combination of cultures in any given congregation is virtually endless.

Each multicultural congregation is unique in its ethnic makeup and approach to ministry and worship. Some congregations are monolingual while others are bilingual and still others are multilingual. Part (or most) of a congregation's ministry may be focused on newly arrived immigrants (documented or undocumented) while another congregation may be multiethnic but composed of persons whose ancestors arrived on this soil several generations ago. Some multicultural churches have numerous persons within their congregations who have recently converted to Christianity and are hearing the biblical stories for the first time. Each congregation has its own challenges and its own ways of honoring and celebrating its diversity and the common Christian tie that binds them together as a faith community.

Cross-Cultural Communication

Communicating in relatively homogenous congregations can be rife with misunderstandings. This becomes even more complicated when communicating across cultures. Often idioms don't translate from one language to another ("It's raining cats and dogs" can be very confusing for those who are studying English as a second language). The same word in English can have a different meaning to a person in Australia or Britain (a "bench" to an Australian is a kitchen "counter" to an American, or the "trunk" of a car is the "boot" for a Briton). The tone of voice (e.g., an ironic tone) can totally change the meaning of a word that may not be understood by those less familiar with the nuances of that particular language. Younger generations have their own vocabulary that often doesn't communicate outside that particular cultural group ("bad" really means "good"). Each culture's value system and worldview forms the basic assumptions that lie behind every communication event, whether it is verbal or nonverbal.

Worship is clearly a communication event, and in multicultural congregations, miscommunication and associated problems can arise when communicating cross-culturally. Chapter 3 will deal with these issues in depth.

Definition of Terms

In addition to communication across cultures being an extremely complicated task, another difficulty in communication lies with a whole new set of words and phrases that have emerged in attempts to talk about multiculturalism. The whole language of multiculturalism is relatively new to the English language and its usage in the United States. If you look at a dictionary from thirty years ago, the word *multiculturalism* will not be listed. And to complicate things even further, people in the fields of anthropology, urban ministry, population growth, or genetics may use the same term to mean different things.

The definitions of terms we thought we understood, such as *race*, are now being challenged. So let me try to clarify what meanings I intend behind the language I use throughout this book.

Race: The problem with the word *race* is that some scientists believe that it is not a helpful category for classifying human beings anymore.

The concept [of race] has little or no value for describing human biological diversity. This is because the pattern of human variation is predominantly one of within-group variation, so that it is impossible to delineate clear boundaries between groups. Biological differences between groups result from the isolation of breeding populations, but evidence indicates contact between groups since at least the Middle Pleistocene (0.6 million years ago). In the past 500 years, with the expansion of trade, colonization, etc., long-range contacts have greatly increased; gene pools are in constant flux, and the biological contrasts between populations are slight, relative to their internal variety.[4]

Basically, the variations within any one traditionally defined "race" are as great as the variations between "races." Still, if we eliminate race from our vocabulary (which is an intriguing idea), then we also eliminate *racism.* And racism is a topic in this country that still needs to be dealt with by everyone. Racism is "the belief that some races are inherently superior (physically, intellectually, or culturally) to others, and therefore have a right to dominate them."[5] Racism has contributed much pain and suffering to numerous groups of people in this country, and much more work needs to be done to overcome our racist attitudes and actions before we can eliminate it from our vocabulary.

However, I will use *race* sparingly. It is used by the United States Bureau of Census, and it is an important distinction in regard to assimilation into another culture. For example, a light-skinned Mexican woman coming to this country at age ten can master the English language and American culture and can be perceived by the dominant culture as white and therefore be treated as an equal.

---

[4]David Crystal, ed., *Cambridge Encyclopedia* (Cambridge: Cambridge University Press, 1997), 885.

[5]E. D. Hirsch, Jr., Joseph F. Kett, and James Trefil, *Dictionary of Cultural Literacy*, 2d ed. (Boston: Houghton Mifflin, 1993), 338.

However, a Japanese man or an African woman who is second- or third-generation American is often born into the American culture learning English as a first language, but neither will be able to "pass" in this country because of their "racial" features.

Biracial means that a person was born to parents of different races. And the term *multiracial* can identify someone whose heritage is a combination of several races: an African American grandfather, a Native American grandmother, a German father, and a Native American/African American mother. The term can also be used to refer to a congregation whose members comprise two or more races.

Ethnicity: Ethnicity is different from race. Ethnicity refers to an "identity with or membership in a particular racial, national, or cultural group, and observance of that group's customs, beliefs, and language."[6] A church can be *monoracial* (an all-black church) but *multiethnic* if there are African American members as well as persons from the Caribbean with African ancestry or Africans from Ghana or Nigeria, Sierra Leone or Zaire. Or a congregation may be composed only of Asians, but they are multiethnic: Koreans, Chinese, Japanese, Taiwanese, and so on.

Ethnocentricism: Ethnocentrism is "the belief that one's own culture is superior to all others, and is the standard by which all other cultures should be measured."[7] In many ways, ethnocentrism is as destructive as racism. The problem with ethnocentrism in this country is that many European Americans are not sufficiently aware of the value systems and intricacies of our own culture to realize we judge all others by it. Some go so far as to say that European Americans have no culture! Herein lies the difficulty. What is a culture?

Culture: Culture is "the sum attitudes, customs, and beliefs that distinguishes one group of people from another. Culture is transmitted through language, material objects, ritual, institutions, and art from one generation to the next."[8] The first part of this definition can refer to numerous groupings of persons. Take youth culture. I certainly don't understand half of their language. I understand the words but not the meanings behind the words. I am clueless about the material objects they insert in and under their skin, and their reasons for piercing their eyebrows, noses, belly buttons, and who knows what else. Their music and other art forms often separate them from other persons.

---

[6]Ibid., 417.
[7]Ibid.
[8]Ibid., 415.

Yet the last part of this definition is about passing down these "sum attitudes, customs, and beliefs" from one generation to the next. For this reason, culture is often used to refer to *ethnic* cultures. Whenever *culture* is used in this book, it will usually refer to *ethnic* cultures unless there is an adjective to clarify its usage for another group of people: Generation X culture, denominational culture, and so on.

The term *bicultural* is used to identify a person who is comfortable moving in and out of two different cultures. For example, most African Americans are bicultural. They know how to adapt their language, behavior patterns, and values from one culture to the other.

The term *multicultural* can be used to identify a person who is comfortable in more than two cultures (many Europeans can move in and out of French, Swiss, British, or German cultures). A congregation is identified as multicultural if its membership is made up of persons from two or more different cultures.

Multiculturalism: Multiculturalism is "the view that the various cultures in a society merit equal respect and scholarly interest."[9] In many ways, this is a fuzzy definition. What does "equal respect" mean? Some interpret this to mean equal treatment, equal authority, and so on. With this interpretation, *multiculturalism* and *ethnocentrism* collide. It is difficult to believe all cultures merit equal treatment and still hold on to an ethnocentric attitude that "my" culture is superior. Others will argue, however, that they can respect another culture while still holding on to the belief that their culture is superior.

Whichever end of the spectrum one leans toward, the role of cultural critique is crucial. Some people are always ready to critique another's culture but are defensive of their own. Others are always critiquing their own culture and "romanticizing" the cultures of others. In reality, however, we need to critique our own culture, and we need to provide some judgments on other cultural practices and beliefs. For example, I want to honor the communal nature of African cultures, their rich dance rituals in worship, and their music, but I do not want to affirm the cultural practice of female circumcision practiced in some countries. Likewise, there are things that I want to uphold about my own culture and things that definitely need to be critiqued and challenged.

In general society the problem is what (or whose) "higher" standard is being used to make these value judgments. In the church we think it is easier because we have a standard by which to do cultural critique—the will of God. But as we saw in the situation in South Africa

---

[9]Ibid., 423.

during apartheid and in this country during slavery, the "will of God" can be interpreted very differently by persons from diverse cultures.

The controversy over the definition of multiculturalism will not be resolved here; neither will the controversy over how to live in a multicultural church, let alone a multicultural society. The conversation will continue in this country for many years to come.[10] For the purposes of this book, however, multiculturalism will be used to refer to the attitude or belief that the cultures present in our society deserve attention and respect. In terms of multicultural congregations, each culture has elements that are sacred and important to the spiritual lives of the people raised in that culture. When these elements can be interpreted for others outside the culture and can be used appropriately and with integrity, the congregation should be open to having these elements shared with the entire congregation.

Assimilation: Assimilation is "the process by which a person or persons acquire the social and psychological characteristics of a group."[11] It is difficult for anyone to achieve educational, social, or career goals in this country without assimilating to some degree to what is called "the American culture" (most often defined by the European American, male powerbase and that which fosters capitalist economics).

Assimilationism, on the other hand, is "a specific ideology that sets the fundamental conditions for full economic and social citizenship in the United States." It has three main features: (1) It "requires adherence to core principles and behaviors"; (2) It "rejects racialized group consciousness"; and (3) It "repudiates cultural equity among groups."[12] Assimilationism in many ways is the opposite of multiculturalism. It views equality among cultures as a threat to harmony and peace.[13] And when you think about it, cultural equity is a logistical nightmare for government and the church. We can't negotiate differences between Republicans and Democrats or Pentecostals and Episcopalians, let alone the numerous cultural groups that make up this country. Multiculturalism is hard work. Total assimilationism is so much easier—at least for those in power.

In reality, assimilation happens on a variety of levels. All immigrant children must assimilate to the American educational system. To one degree or another, we all assimilate to the values and

---

[10]For a more detailed discussion, see Avery F. Gordon and Christopher Newfield, eds., *Mapping Multiculturalism* (Minneapolis: University of Minnesota Press, 1996).

[11]Hirsch et al., *Dictionary of Cultural Literacy,* 412.

[12]Gordon and Newfield, *Mapping Multiculturalism,* 80.

[13]Ibid., 81.

practices of the Western-style medical establishment. We talk about the "Southwest" as if it had a culture all its own, and in reality it does, because most people in that region have assimilated the various ways of the Native American inhabitants as well as the Mexican American population and the European American peoples. A new "Southwest" culture has been created out of the mix. And in many multicultural churches, a "new" culture has been created out of their interaction and the living out of the gospel among the diverse members.

But what about the term *multicultural worship?*

- Does multicultural worship identify the worship of any congregation that is multicultural in its makeup?
- Or does multicultural worship identify the form and content of worship rather than the people present in the congregation?
- Can multiculturalism happen (each culture is given equal respect) in worship when the form, content, style, and tone of worship is the same as it was when the congregation was homogenous?
- Or should the service itself (at one time or another, depending on what model is being used) be representative of the various cultures present?
- Can a worship service be multicultural in an all-white congregation in Nebraska?

These questions do not have easy answers. Designing worship in a multicultural context is still a relatively new field. It is that odd creature that is both ancient and new, familiar yet strange, enticing yet possibly dangerous. The term *multicultural worship* can be confusing, depending on who is using it.

Taken in its broadest sense, multicultural worship can refer to a large spectrum of worship practice. At one end of the spectrum is worship with absolutely no changes made to accommodate the new cultures represented in the multicultural congregation. The newer members are expected to fully assimilate into the existing worship style.

At the other end of the spectrum is the type of worship that is done at World Council of Churches meetings. In these worship services, a song from South Africa is sung in Zulu, a sung response is taken from the Greek Orthodox Church, the corporate prayer of confession was written by someone in Brazil, and the scripture is read in the Tagalog language of the Philippines. While these liturgies are very multicultural, they are designed for a large group of people who come together for a short period of time, not for a continuing worshiping community.

In between these extremes are a wide variety of models that vary in the way churches incorporate the spiritualities and worship traditions of the cultures present in their congregations.

I do not need to describe or analyze the worship that happens at the end of the spectrum where the church is multicultural in its membership but the worship has not changed. It is "the way it has always been." Because the congregation is multicultural, some would argue that their worship is multicultural as well. Because of the differences of opinion surrounding the meaning of the term *multicultural,* it is difficult to articulate the other models on this spectrum.

What I would like to address are those churches that are trying to take cultural diversity seriously in designing worship. I do not want to deny the term *multicultural worship* to any congregation that is multicultural. On the other hand, I want to distinguish between those congregations that assimilate persons of other cultures into the traditional worship of that congregation and those that intentionally design worship to be inclusive of the diversity of cultures represented in the congregation. I have chosen another phrase to describe the latter: *culturally-conscious worship.*

Culturally-Conscious Worship: The design of culturally-conscious worship intentionally works with a consciousness of:

1. our multiracial, multiethnic, and multicultural society and world
2. the cultural diversity (its gifts and challenges) present in the congregation
3. persons who experience living on the margins and living with inequity of power.

Number 3 in the above definition can refer to persons of any ethnicity. This is intentional, since projections for the future also suggest that class or economic status will be the determining dividing factor of the future rather than race or ethnicity.[14] The "cultural" experience of the lower classes is already something the church should be addressing. Culturally-conscious worship takes these subcultures seriously as well.

---

[14]*Race in America: A Message from LA.* Video production of the Multicultural Collaborative, 1998. Distributed by Dubs Inc., 1220 N. Highland Ave., Hollywood, CA, 90038.

Culturally-Conscious Worship

This book, *Culturally-Conscious Worship,* is just one of many contributions to the dialogue of what it means to be a multicultural faith community. It is by no means a definitive statement on multiculturalism or worship or any combination of the two. It is not a recipe book for culturally-conscious worship, since each church's context (denomination, cultures represented in the congregation, pastoral leadership, lay leadership, etc.) is so very different.

Instead, this book tries to lay out some of the cultural and liturgical issues that pastors may face when designing worship in a multicultural context. Hopefully, you will gain a deeper awareness and sensitivity of the underlying factors that contribute to communication across cultures.

In worship, communication happens on a variety of levels. Sometimes what we intend to communicate and what people receive are at cross purposes because we are unaware of the cultural assumptions that form both the intent of a message and the reception of any verbal or nonverbal communication.

- Do some members of the congregation arrive twenty to thirty minutes late to church? Is this interpreted by some to be disrespectful?
- Does the Sharing of Joys and Concerns seem to go on too long? Whose cultural assumptions are deciding what is "too long"?
- Is music style a continual hot topic of controversy? Whose cultural biases determine what music is appropriate for sacred settings?
- Are the aisles congested during the Passing of the Peace or Ritual of Friendship because people refuse to stay in their pews to greet one another?
- Are you struggling with the issue of Sunday worship being worship or evangelism?
- Is there conversation about which prayers are more spiritual—corporate prayers printed in the bulletin or an extemporaneous prayer offered by someone on behalf of the congregation?
- Is there conflict over who is responsible for disciplining children?
- Are some people uncomfortable being called by their first names?
- Are some people complaining that worship is going on too long?

- Are some saying that your sermons are too short and others that they are too long?

Each of these questions and many, many more all have (often unconscious) cultural assumptions that lie behind the communication event. Some have to do with cultural differences about time (being "on time" or "wasting time"). Some have to do with cultural definitions of what a sermon is and isn't, what sacred music should sound like, or what kinds of prayers God prefers. Others have to do with issues of formality and informality and what is appropriate in a sacred setting. (These issues will be dealt with in depth in chapter 3.)

In reality, the controversies named above can be found in homogenous congregations among people of the same ethnicity but who come from different geographical regions, different denominational backgrounds, or different generations. We don't think that the cultural differences of "the South" or "the West" or denominational or generational cultures make that big a difference, but communication and liturgical expectations can be conflicts in homogenous congregations as well.

In multicultural congregations, geographical, denominational, theological, and liturgical differences, along with generational differences, are complicated by ethnic cultural differences and often linguistic differences as well. As persons from various cultures bring their own expectations about the form, content, style, and mood or "feel" of worship, negotiating these differences can be quite a challenge.

Predictions of the Future

If the projections of the United States Bureau of Census statistics for future population growth are correct, chances are multicultural congregations will increase in number over the next fifty years rather than decrease. Keeping in mind the concerns about the definition of "race" today, but recognizing that this is still how our government classifies people, let us look at the statistics.

Based on birth and death rates in the various ethnic communities, population statistics predict that by the year 2050:

- The European American (white) population will increase by 3 percent.
- The black race (of any nationality: African Americans, Nigerians, Jamaicans) will increase by 69 percent.
- American Indians, Eskimos, and Aleuts will increase in population by 79.5 percent.

- Asians and Pacific Islanders will increase 195 percent.
- Hispanics (of numerous nationalities) will increase in population 199 percent.[15]

I realize that for some European Americans, maybe even some African Americans, these numbers stir within them a sense of anxiety, even fear. The rhinoceros horns on the creature of my dream loom more large and threatening than its cuddly shaggy dog possibilities. European Americans will only increase their population by 3 percent. Asians and Hispanics will triple in population while the African American population will increase by just over fifty percent. While blacks outnumber Hispanics at the turn of the new millennium, by 2050 there will be 96,508,000 Hispanics and only 60,592,000 persons of African descent.[16]

But to the Christian church, these numbers should not be met with disdain or contempt or even fear and trembling, because the largest growing churches are often among these populations. Many come with a rich Christian heritage, a celebrative spirit, and a deep commitment to both God and neighbor.

The future is ripe with excitement as we share our faith journeys and ritual practices with one another. This is not to say that languages won't be stumbling blocks, or that differing theologies won't pose problems, or that a true welcome from all sides will be easy. Although we are often aware of surface differences between persons of one culture and another (the names people give their children, the food they eat, what they wear to church, the music they listen to, the way they greet one another), we are often unaware of the deeper differences that divide cultures based on worldviews and value systems.

These deeper issues can cause difficulties when communicating cross-culturally—especially in worship. There will be many challenges to face in the coming years as we all work together to overcome our various ethnocentric attitudes and behaviors. Still, we are all one in the body of Christ, and the future of the church and our society may depend on how we meet this multicultural challenge.

Sneak Previews

In the text that follows, chapter 1 examines the various motivations churches have for becoming multicultural and the motivations individuals have for joining a multicultural congregation.

---

[15]United States Bureau of Census Web site (www.census.gov).
[16]Ibid.

Understanding the role worship plays or doesn't play in personal decisions to become a member of a multicultural congregation will help us in the design of culturally-conscious worship. Then various models of culturally-conscious worship will be explored.

Chapter 2 provides a theological and biblical foundation for what we do in culturally-conscious worship and the way ethnocentric and racist attitudes work against living out our faith in a multicultural world.

Chapter 3 examines a number of cultural differences that can create problems in both the design and implementation of culturally-conscious worship. Issues of time, rhythm, personal space, power sharing, formality and informality, care of children, individualism, and communal commitments, among other concerns, will all be explored.

Chapter 4 explores a theology of worship: What is worship? What is the purpose of worship in your congregation? It then analyzes the need for developing a shared story, a shared memory in multicultural congregations, and looks at ways to elicit individual stories in worship.

Chapter 5 describes some liturgical foundations for keeping balance in the design and content of worship when changes are made to be inclusive of the cultures represented in the congregation.

The intent of this book is to map out the landscape of worship in multicultural congregations, to ascertain what some of the underlying issues are, and to begin the conversation about what it means to worship in a multicultural context. What follows is an exploration of this strange but fascinating creature called *culturally-conscious worship*.

CHAPTER ONE

Motivations and Models

As we look toward designing worship in a multicultural context that is culturally conscious, it is important to ascertain why churches were motivated to become multicultural, why individuals have chosen to join a multicultural congregation, and what models currently exist for culturally-conscious worship.

Motivations for Churches

Multicultural congregations are becoming a reality in most cities and even small towns in this country. The reasons churches are multicultural are varied. Some congregations are strong, but they have a large building that is not fully utilized and welcome another congregation (e.g., a European American congregation welcomes a Korean congregation or an African American congregation welcomes a Hispanic congregation) to share their facilities. Others are smaller congregations who are struggling financially and rent space to another congregation to help pay the bills. During the year, however, the two congregations often worship together for special occasions.

There are other congregations that find themselves in a changing neighborhood. Most of the members have moved out of the immediate area. Fewer and fewer of the long-time members are willing or able to commute to church every Sunday, let alone participate in activities during the week. The leaders realize that if they don't open their doors to persons of other cultures, the church may close. Some do this reluctantly, but others see this as a wonderful opportunity for evangelism and outreach to the surrounding community to bring people to Christ.

For many congregations, however, becoming multicultural just happened without a lot of thought or planning. One Filipino family started coming, and they invited their friends and extended family members, and after a while one fourth of the congregation was Filipino. Or in an African American congregation, an African family joined as did a family from Jamaica, and over time, several more African and Caribbean families joined the church.

In most of these congregations, the worship life of the congregation has not changed because the cultural makeup of the congregation has changed. It is assumed that the people come because they are comfortable in the worship service and receive meaning and grace from it. Since becoming multicultural was not an intentional plan by the pastor(s) or lay leaders, life went on as usual. However, when a new pastor is appointed or called to (what is now) a multicultural congregation, she or he may wonder what difference a multicultural context makes in the planning, design, content, structure, and leadership of worship.

There are a few congregations that have made intentional decisions to become multicultural because they believe God's plan is for equality of all people and that the church should lead the way in showing the world how different cultures can live, work, and worship together. They struggle with what this means for the design, content, and style of worship. They know that the presence of diverse cultures has an impact on worship, but what changes that entails is often a continuing process of discernment.[1]

Motivations for Individuals

Churches don't always have the choice of whether or not to become multicultural. When individuals decide they want to join a particular church, the church can make it very clear that they are not welcome, but few churches barricade their doors anymore with signs saying "Whites only" or "Blacks only" or "Koreans only." So it is important to understand why persons would choose to join a congregation that is predominantly of a culture other than their own or why persons choose to join a multicultural congregation. While

---

[1]Charles Foster, in his book *Embracing Diversity: Leadership in Multicultural Congregations* (Washington, D.C.: Alban Institute, 1997), identifies four "catalysts" that cause congregations to become multicultural: (1) quest for survival, (2) gospel commitment, (3) hospitality, and (4) theological vision. For a more detailed account, see pp. 8–11.

the reasons are as numerous and different as the individuals involved, some common motivations can be identified.

1. *Integration.* The Brown versus Board of Education Supreme Court decision for forced integration happened in 1954. The civil rights movement of Martin Luther King, Jr., was in full swing by the mid-'60s. After that, there were some African Americans who wanted to claim their right to full integration in this society in restaurants, on buses, in schools, and in churches.

   At that time, integration meant assimilation. If you were welcome at all, you had to abide by the rules, style of worship, music choices, and channels of authority of the dominant culture. You could join if you didn't make any demands and acted like "us." And while there were some African Americans who chose to join all-white churches (for whatever reasons), other African Americans accused them of "running from their blackness," of betraying their community, of being an "oreo"– black on the outside but white on the inside. Whatever their internal motivations were, African Americans pioneered the integration of some European American congregations in the 1960s and 1970s.

2. *Assimilation.* Some immigrant groups who came to this country chose to join European American congregations where they could polish their English skills and learn the cultural norms of their new country. As newcomers to the United States, they were trying to "fit in." They basically assumed that they had no power in their new context (e.g., to ask the pastor to accommodate some of their worship needs) and made the necessary compromises and adaptations necessary for worshiping in a foreign environment. It was socially and economically helpful for them to make contacts with persons from the majority culture and to improve their English skills. Being in a Christian faith community gave them a sense of commonality and familiarity in a culture foreign to them.

3. *Denominational Loyalty.* While denominational loyalty is decreasing in the United States, it can still be found among persons who immigrate to this country. This is especially true of Episcopalians/Anglicans and Roman Catholics, although it is present in nonliturgical denominations as well. Jamaicans may seek out the closest Disciples of Christ church, even though it is an all-white congregation, because they were

Disciples of Christ in Jamaica. Or persons from Vietnam or Laos or Cambodia may seek out a Christian Missionary Alliance Church because that denomination had the strongest missionary influence in Southeast Asia. Persons from Ghana may seek out a United Methodist congregation because they were Methodists in Ghana.

Denominational loyalty may also be influenced by a particular "characteristic" of the denomination. In Pentecostal churches, speaking in tongues is an important characteristic. This "gift of the spirit" has the power to unite persons from different ethnic and cultural backgrounds.

4. *Linguistic or Racial Bonds.* Persons from various cultures may choose a particular congregation because of the language that is used in worship (Puerto Ricans and Guatemalans worshiping together in Spanish, or deaf persons from various cultures worshiping together in sign language).

Or the congregation may be multicultural because of racial (though not ethnic or cultural) commonality: Africans joining an African American congregation or Navajo, Creek, and Sioux worshiping together.

5. *Acceptance.* For a variety of reasons, some people don't feel accepted in the churches of their own culture. This is especially true of many gay and lesbian persons, but it may also be true of persons who are divorced, persons with disabilities, ex-prisoners, and so on. For gays and lesbians, there are few churches that accept them as active participants in the life of the congregation if they are open about their sexual orientation. The churches that welcome them with open arms may be of a different culture than their own.

6. *Making a Difference.* Multicultural congregations are seldom without needs of one sort or another, and some persons are drawn to this type of community. They feel their presence can make a difference. They are needed in this body of Christ, and the congregation is open and welcoming of the contributions they have to offer.

7. *Multicultural Environment.* Many middle-aged and young adults today have been raised in multiethnic public schools and colleges; they work in multiethnic environments, exercise together in multiethnic gyms, and participate in numerous social and recreational clubs that are multiethnic in their make-up. They choose a multiethnic, multicultural environment in which to worship as well. Parents may choose to raise their

children in a multicultural spiritual environment so that their children can handle the conflicts that inevitably arise in the classroom or on the playground between persons of different ethnic and cultural backgrounds.

There are also persons whose core family or core being is multicultural: those in "mixed marriages," adult children born to a mixed couple, and those parents who have adopted children from other cultures. A multicultural faith community allows biracial or multiracial individuals, both spouses of a mixed marriage, or parents with adopted children to feel as if they fully belong. No one stands out as "different."

8. *Justice Oriented.* There are people from a wide variety of cultures who are convinced that the biblical mandate to strive for justice and peace on this earth requires people to cross boundaries, to negotiate differences, and to work toward a sense of well-being for all. They do not support the assimilation model but rather want both the richness and the challenge of sharing their faith journeys with persons whose spiritual paths are rooted in languages and soils, rituals and prayers of a different land or culture. They want to be changed by the interchange, to be reformed by new insights, to be inspired by new rhythms and songs.

As our society becomes more multicultural, there is a sense of urgency. If we cannot learn how to be truly multicultural in the church—each shaping the other and creating a common culture from the mix—we cannot expect peace across ethnicities and justice across cultures for our society, let alone the world. Persons join congregations expecting that their presence will make a difference, that their cultural affinities will challenge some of the status quo, that their racial heritage will affect some of the power dynamics in the church, and that their "liturgical homeland" and expressions of spirituality will influence the form and content of worship.

9. *Geographical Proximity.* Particularly in Roman Catholic parishes, people (of whatever ethnicity) attend the parish closest to them. Others choose the closest neighborhood church (regardless of predominant ethnicity) because they don't own a car and can walk or take public transportation to the church.

This list is not exhaustive of why persons choose a multicultural congregation, but it is representative of the historical and contemporary factors that have created multicultural faith communities today. While worship may be one's initial contact with any given congregation (although in immigrant communities it may be English as a Second Language [ESL] classes), it is not necessarily the reason why persons stay. There are numerous factors that contribute to a person's deciding to join a multicultural congregation.

Those who in the past sought integration, those in the past and present who seek assimilation into this country, those who cherish the acceptance they receive, and those who join because of linguistic or racial bonds may not care greatly whether the worship style best expresses the rhythms, prayer forms, moods, and proclamations of their "liturgical homeland." Their spiritual and social fulfillment comes in other ways, through other avenues of the church's life and ministry. And over time they often grow into this new worship style in the same way that we all have adapted to and grown into liturgical reform over the years.

Those who join because of denominational loyalty, or who want a multicultural environment, or who seek a justice community may easily adapt to whatever worship style is currently practiced at a particular church. Many persons of minority cultures are accustomed to feeling powerless to change the status quo and are accustomed to adjusting and compromising their needs and preferences to the dominant culture's preexisting patterns (in this case, worship patterns). The basic pattern of worship of the particular denomination, the multicultural environment, or a congregation's commitment to justice and peace in other aspects of its mission and ministry may be sufficient to sustain them spiritually.

However, it is also possible that persons who join for these reasons want to feel a familiar beat. They may want to receive communion in a certain posture and feel the Spirit's energy moving throughout the congregation in the way that they experienced in their own culture and faith. And just as European Americans were inspired to share the message of Christ through their cultural style of worship with people around the world (sometimes in destructive ways), persons from other cultures want to share their knowledge of Christ in their lives. They want to share their worship styles, their inspirations, their testimonies, and their rhythms with their multicultural congregations.

Models of Culturally-Conscious Worship

My goal was to identify the various processes that went into designing culturally-conscious worship. I suspected that the "end product"—the worship service itself—would be unique to each congregation and hence not transferable. There were too many factors to take into consideration, such as the cultures present in the congregation, the pastoral and lay leadership, and the denominational background(s) of the pastor and lay members. Therefore, I was more interested in what decisions were made, how they were made, and by whom, that led to the culturally-conscious worship experience.

One assumption that proved false was that the worship life of the congregation was the important critical factor in establishing and maintaining a strong multicultural congregation, since worship is often a person's first entry into a congregation. But, as I have noted above, worship may not be the determining factor as to whether a person comes to a multicultural church, joins the church, or stays active in the church. Pastoral care, fellowship, education (religious education and ESL classes) for themselves and their children, commitment to global issues, commitment to justice issues, theology, hospitality, and commitment to a multicultural community may all be strong contributing factors to a person's decision.

Nonetheless, worship is an important weekly event in every congregation. Many come to worship who do not attend any other regular activity that the church offers. And worship has the power not only to attract people and to keep them as regular participants, but also to shape the lives of individuals as well as the faith community on their spiritual journey together. And shaping a multicultural community is not an easy task.

So, what processes go into making decisions about the final form and content of culturally-conscious worship? In many churches, these processes emerged over time and are still emerging. Initially, as persons from other cultures join a particular congregation, the worship usually stays the same. The basic assumption is that "they" (those of another culture) like what they see and experience in worship and therefore keep coming. This may be a false assumption, as I have noted above.

Over time, however, there may be sufficient numbers of the "minority"[2] culture to have not only a voice but also a vote in the decision-making processes about the daily operations of the life of the church, including its worship. Or a new pastor may be called or appointed to the church who was not a part of the congregation when it slowly became multicultural. She or he may want to take seriously the cultural makeup of the congregation and make changes in the

---

[2]I have struggled with the negative implications of the terms *minority* and *majority* but have found no other vocabulary to identify numerical differentials. While I realize that greater numbers usually means greater power and these terms can be laden with subordinate/dominant, inferior/superior connotations, I would like to use *minority* and *majority* to talk about population size.

form, content, or "feel" of the liturgy to be more representative of the various cultures present in the congregation. Or, for theological and justice reasons, a congregation may make intentional decisions about changing or adapting their worship in a way that is representative of the spiritualities, ritual practices, rhythms, and prayer forms found in the faith journeys of the people of various cultures in the congregation.

The process of decision making and the final design and content of the worship service varies from congregation to congregation, but there are some "models" that can be identified.

Inherited Liturgy Provides the Design. In some denominations the basis of the liturgy is predetermined by some sort of liturgical resource: Book of Common Prayer, Book of Worship, Missal, and so on. In these denominations, the form of the liturgy and often the content of many of the prayers and responses are set. The scripture texts are usually taken from a lectionary, which provides the readings for every liturgical occasion. The choice of music, the instruments used to accompany the music, the visual images present in the environment, and the pastor's sermon provide the degree to which the multicultural makeup of the church is expressed. In some churches, the various racial and cultural constituencies within the congregation seem to have little influence on these "changeable" aspects of worship. In other churches, however, these aspects of the liturgy express the rhythms and spirituality of the diverse people present.

Pastor Designs. This model can be found in a variety of settings. The pastor is basically responsible for the design and leadership of worship so she or he decides the structure, content, and style of worship. This model is often found in congregations where the worship committees are either nonexistent or function more as altar guilds (and occasionally as advisors) than as worship committees.

Historically, this model fostered total assimilation by anyone who wanted to participate in the worship life of the congregation. The pastor designed the service and everyone who came (of whatever ethnicity or culture) either accepted it (or put up with it) and stayed, or rejected it and went elsewhere. This model is used in many multicultural congregations today where the worship is not culturally conscious, but rather still looks and feels "white."

However, this model can also be found in congregations in which a sizable percentage of the membership emigrated from cultures where democracy was not part of the political or ecclesial structure. In many countries, equal representation or participation in decision making is not valued or practiced. It is difficult to get persons from these cultures to actively voice their opinions in regard to worship design and content. They are accustomed to the pastor having autocratic power. It is expected that the pastor will make the decisions, and the congregation will obediently follow.

When the congregation gives total power to the pastor, the design of worship can range from assimilation to culturally-conscious worship. Much depends on the gifts and skills and sensitivities of the pastor. A pastor may decide that to be more inclusive of the cultures represented in the congregation, new music needs to be introduced with different rhythms as well as lyrics that convey the cultural background and spiritual expressions of the cultures represented in the congregation. The pastor solicits favorite hymns/songs from persons of different cultures in the congregation. These hymns may be totally unfamiliar to the congregation, or they may be Western hymns that were adapted by missionaries to the unique rhythms of the new Christian community.

The pastor may decide to introduce Sharing of Joys and Concerns into the liturgy or some form of Passing of the Peace so that shared bonding might happen between people of different cultures. The pastor may use corporate printed prayers one week and ask someone from the congregation to give an extemporaneous prayer the next week to balance the prayer forms that are most common in the traditions represented in the congregation.

Obviously, the people will give the pastor feedback on any changes that are made to the "way it has always been done," and the pastor will then make additional decisions about whether to continue certain practices, introduce some at a slower pace, or eliminate some of the new elements altogether. The decisions about the design, content, and "feel" of the service, however, are made almost entirely by the pastor.

While this may seem autocratic, it is a model that can work and work well in some contexts. There are some churches where the laity of the majority culture don't want to make any changes to accommodate the persons of other cultures, and there are other churches where nobody understands the issues, and the people don't see multicultural worship as an important need. There are also church members of the minority culture who experience themselves as powerless to *ask* for change, let alone *effect* any change in the content or style of worship.

By having total control over the design and content of the liturgy, the pastor can push people beyond the status quo and their comfort zones. It nudges the majority culture to compromise elements of their "liturgical homeland" and open themselves up to the rich spiritual traditions of another. It nudges the minority culture(s) to risk sharing their music and prayers and ritual practices with a majority culture they perceive as self-sufficient, neither needing nor wanting anything from anyone.

Professional Team Designs. The professional team usually consists of the clergy, professional musicians, song leader, and persons in charge of drama, liturgical dance, or other art forms. This model can be found in many "contemporary worship" services or "seeker services." It is important to note that the professional team, often called the worship team, is not usually representative of the various cultures in the congregation. Rather, whoever plays the guitar, or drums, or saxophone, or keyboard is a member of the team regardless of ethnicity.

In some of these contexts, worship can be very "performance" oriented rather than participatory. The worship team performs the liturgy for the people. In seeker services, this may be intentional, so that those who are seeking an expression of their spirituality are not pressured into participating in something that is still uncomfortable for them.

This model, however, is also found at various ecumenical gatherings where worship usually opens or closes the meetings. It is also used in large multicultural gatherings such as the World Council of Churches liturgies. The form, content, structure, music, other art forms, and symbolic actions are designed by a team of professional liturgical "artists." These liturgical artists may or may not be representative of the cultures of the participants in the liturgy. With persons from so many cultures present at the World Council of Churches meetings, it would be almost impossible to have representatives from them all.

In these contexts, the liturgies are usually carefully planned in advance and "choreographed." The team intentionally chooses music from various cultures and denominational traditions. They often vary the instruments that will be used to accompany the hymns/songs. The visual environment, the use of symbols, the design of the altar, and the position of the seating are all taken into consideration so that a complex communication event such as worship in a global setting can be conveyed on multiple levels around a particular theme or text.

Often there is a rehearsal or at least a detailed "walkthrough" of each worship service in order to anticipate any problems with the design, possible interruptions to the flow of the service, sudden shifts in mood or tone, offensive language (especially in interfaith services but also in ecumenical services), and so on. When any kind of symbolic action is being used, the design team must consider the logistics of getting people out of their seats and back again as well as any possible problem the symbols may create (e.g., carrying a lighted candle). Since those who create the service often recruit a representative group of people to lead the service, the rehearsal also facilitates a smooth transition from one liturgical leader to the next, from one liturgical element to the next.

These services are excellent models of culturally-conscious and ecumenical worship. The same model can be used on a smaller scale in the local church, but it requires much time and preparation. Good culturally-conscious worship may not come easily or quickly; many find this model extremely time intensive. Often it is difficult (but not impossible) to gather the kind of "liturgical artists" necessary for such an undertaking on a weekly basis. However, a pastor or congregation can begin training several laypersons, who are interested in worship design and planning, to become this worship team in the future.

Representative Committee Designs. In this model, a worship committee is intentionally chosen to be representative of the various cultures present in the congregation. This model *can* function along the lines of tokenism. One person from the minority cultures represented in the congregation is appointed to the worship committee. This lone voice seldom has the power to influence any decision. In reality, life and worship usually go on as usual.

This model, however, can be exciting and challenging when several persons from each culture represented in the congregation are members of the worship committee. By including more than one representative of a culture, the subgroup is more apt to feel equal, with a sense of power. The challenging part is negotiating the differences that will inevitably arise. Each individual, each cultural group, and the worship committee as a whole will have to decide which elements of worship are negotiable and which are not. Then compromises will need to be made on all sides.

The exciting part of this model is that the cultural representatives on the committee share information from their various cultures with the committee. The committee learns about the faith journeys of one another and the elements of worship that are most meaningful to them, such as the music and rhythms that inspire their souls, the way they pray, and the cultural symbols that have become Christian symbols. As the committee empathizes with the moods and emotions that characterize worship at the core of the others' being, the committee can devise powerful and meaningful ways to share these with the congregation.

As various elements from the different cultures are introduced into worship, it is natural for some to be "put up with" or even opposed, but inevitably, others are adopted by the whole congregation. A song from Africa makes a deep connection with people across cultures; reading the scripture in another language (with the text also printed in English in the bulletin) allows the congregation to hear the rhythms and vocal inflections of a language that is so dear to some of its members. Everyone may learn a few songs in different languages. A prayer form used in Pakistan may be tried and appreciated as a layperson is asked to pray from their seat on behalf of the congregation. Or the Korean custom of the Tong Song Kido prayer, in which everyone prays his or her own prayer aloud simultaneously, may become accepted by the entire congregation.

Over time, what emerges is a new style of worship where various elements of different cultures are included in worship on a regular basis. In a way, a "third" culture is created that combines some of the values, ritual practices, and rhythms of the cultures represented in the congregation. Visitors may not be totally comfortable at first, but hopefully they will find some elements in the worship that speak directly to them.

Various Worship Groups Design. Another model honors the diversity present in the congregation in a different way. Rather than having one worship committee that is representative of the congregation that designs a "blended" style of worship, this model utilizes a variety of worship "groups" to design each Sunday's service.

Dumbarton United Methodist Church in the Georgetown area of Washington, D.C., is one representative of this model. They have a worship committee (called the Worship Cluster) that is composed of the pastor, the chair of the Worship Cluster, the artist-in-residence, the music director, and the person responsible for creating a visual environment in the sanctuary that reflects the various liturgical seasons. While the Worship Cluster is a coordinating body for Sunday services, it does not design the weekly worship services. Sunday services are designed by several groups of laity who each take responsibility for worship on a particular Sunday.

For Dumbarton, the process often begins with a half-day gathering or an overnight retreat (open to anyone interested) to look over the Sundays of a particular liturgical season or a particular period of time (the month of July, the six weeks of Lent, or a series on a particular text, topic, or biblical character, for example). The group discusses the lectionary texts, issues facing the congregation, and topics of concern that might provide the foundation for worship in the coming weeks. Cultural occasions such as the Fourth of July, Mother's Day, and Martin Luther King, Jr.'s, birthday, as well as congregational events such as a work team going to Nicaragua are also taken into consideration.

Those present at the retreat go through an overview of the season/period of weeks to be planned and then some sort of centering process. After that, the people present are divided up into small groups (usually two to four people each)–one for each Sunday to be planned. These smaller groups then study the four lectionary texts assigned to their Sunday, the themes of the liturgical season, and any other topic relevant to their particular day. The goal is to discover what theme or themes emerge for the group as they study the various texts and topics. The discoveries of each group are then shared with the whole group, and a general image or theme is collectively decided upon that will provide a common link through that season or time period.

Members present at this planning retreat then volunteer to work on the worship design team for a particular Sunday or series of Sundays. Each worship design team (composed of two to four people) is self-selected based on their interest in the liturgical season or the texts, or their availability for a particular day or period. These groups may or may not be racially or culturally mixed.

Each team designs the liturgy, picks the hymns and other music, and writes the Call to Worship, prayers, benedictions, litanies, and so on. Some members of the design team may write lyrics to a familiar tune for a particular service or compose a new song. The team also decides who they want to present the children's storytime and who they want to preach the sermon for their Sunday. Sometimes it is the pastor of the congregation and sometimes not! Each group puts their own interests, preferences, theologies, and personalities into the worship service(s) they design. They may ask others to join them in the designing stage, or the original team may design the liturgy and recruit others in the congregation to be liturgists or scripture readers for their particular Sunday.

The diversity that is representative of the congregation comes through on a week-by-week basis rather than by the creation of a "third" or unique style of worship that was designed for that particular group of people (as in the fourth model, Representative Committee). In this model, worship can be very different from one week to the next. A particular structure or order of worship is encouraged to maintain some continuity, and the general theme that emerged at the retreat is present, but both these elements are flexible and often change. For example, instead of singing the entire hymn before the scripture readings, the hymn verses may be alternated with each scripture reading. Or instead of one person giving the sermon, the preacher of the day may raise the issues found in the texts but then open it up for members of the congregation to share how those texts or issues have affected their lives.

About 20 percent of the congregation has participated in these worship design teams over the years. The team draws on the gifts and graces of many laypersons. Worship is seldom dull, because it changes from week to week. It takes diversity seriously by engaging as many people as possible in the planning and implementation of worship. People "own" worship in a different sense because they have invested their time and talents in its creation.

For visitors, this model of culturally-conscious worship may be exciting or it may be confusing. Since worship is different from week to week, visitors need to come for several months before they decide whether this style of worship fulfills their spiritual needs. Many like the "surprise" that each week has to offer and look forward with anticipation to the new ways God may be revealed to them.

Dumbarton's membership is well educated in both the secular and theological worlds. In a different context, this model may pose problems for persons for whom English is a second language. They may feel uncomfortable writing liturgies in English or may feel that they don't have the training or skills necessary to be on one of the design teams. Having training sessions or mentors (persons who have served on previous design teams) to foster the participation of new members or persons who are hesitant can help to overcome some of these reservations.

A variation of this model can be found in many seminary, hospital, and nursing home chapel services. Worship may also be different from week to week depending on who is responsible for the service that week. In some seminary chapels, there may be a Korean service one week, a Unitarian service the next, and an African American service the next. In hospital and nursing home chapels, the responsibility of weekly worship often rotates among various ministers in the area. One week the Roman Catholic priest will lead the service, the Disciples of Christ minister the next, a Lutheran pastor the next. This results in a wide variety of worship orders, content, and style depending on the ethnicity, culture, and denominational affiliation of the pastor.

Homogenous Context but Culturally-Conscious Worship. This model does not fit neatly into a clearly defined preparation process. In many ways, this model can utilize all the preparation methods listed above except for the fourth model, where a culturally diverse congregation is necessary.

This model reflects those congregations in communities that are not yet culturally diverse or where segregating into one's own cultural community for Sunday morning worship is still the norm.

Some homogenous congregations are extremely aware of the multicultural nature of our world, are committed to global issues of justice, are extremely conscious of the unequal power dynamics that exist, and want to do what they can to fight racism and ethnocentrism. In these congregations, liturgical resources from various cultures are included in worship, visual and musical arts play a prominent role in the worship setting, and concerns of various groups in this country and around the world are lifted up in prayer. Persons of other cultures are not physically present, but their spiritual presence is held up in this unique form of culturally-conscious worship.

Another example may be found in a homogenous Japanese (or some other culture) congregation. The church is homogenous because worship is conducted in their native language. But still they are very conscious of the cultural diversity around them and their own issues of ethnocentrism and racism, and they utilize a variety of resources (translated into Japanese or not) in attempts to design worship that is culturally conscious.

One danger to this is a congregation that utilizes (some would say misappropriates) liturgical resources from other cultures without any commitment to multiculturalism or to dealing with their own racism and ethnocentrism. One Latina seminary student is sometimes asked to read part of the Acts 2 text in Spanish on Pentecost Sunday. The congregation wants to have various verses read in different languages. She refuses to participate because, as a Latina, she knows that on the other fifty-one Sundays of the year she is not welcome.

Models of Bilingual/Multilingual Worship

The multicultural makeup of some congregations necessitates conducting the worship service in two or more languages. In many of these churches, there is often one dominant language. In a Chinese church, Cantonese may be the predominant language, but the services may also be interpreted into Putonghua (Mandarin). In a Filipino church, the worship may be conducted in English, but Tagalog, Ilocano, or Pampango may also be used. How translation happens in bilingual or multilingual worship services varies.

Simultaneous Translation. With simultaneous translation, the other language is often not audible to those who are not accessing the translation. An interpreter voices the translation into a microphone for persons wearing a receiving device (usually from an FM system or an Infrared Assistive Listening System). The interpreter may be in a balcony, in another room with sound played into it, or in a corner of the sanctuary. In some congregations this simultaneous translation takes place throughout the entire worship service. In other congregations, however, it is only the sermon that is translated simultaneously.

Bilingual Translation. In churches that use bilingual translation, various elements (e.g., prayers, sermon, announcements) are given in both languages one after another. If the prayer is short and the person offering the prayer is bilingual, the person praying may speak first in one language and then in the other. When the person praying is not bilingual or not comfortable speaking one of the languages in public, a translator or interpreter will translate the prayer. For long prayers and for the sermon, the translation often takes place "concept after concept." This means that it is not phrase-by-phrase or even sentence-by-sentence translation, but rather a particular concept, the translation, and then the next "concept." These "concept" parameters are very fluid and may be one word or one emphatic phrase, but often it is a longer idea.

Sporadic Translation. There are some churches that only translate a certain element in worship. The children's sermon may be given in English when the rest of the service is conducted in a native language. Or the liturgy is in the English language, with an English bulletin that includes the call to worship, prayers, and so on, but the sermon is translated into the native tongue. The assumption is that people comprehend English when it is printed (in the bulletin, Bible, or hymnal) but prefer their native language for oral reception of the sermon.

Printed Translation. In churches that use some form of printed translation, the translation may be found in the bulletin, worship book, or hymnal. For example, in a Haitian church, there may be a Creole hymnal, a French hymnal, and an English hymnal. Or in a Ghanaian church, there may be a hymnal in Fanti and one in English. Or in some of the newer denominational hymnals, there are Spanish hymns with English translations. During the singing of hymns, individuals in the congregation sing in whatever language is most comfortable.

In a predominantly English-speaking congregation, the scripture may be read in Korean. In that situation, the English translation of the text would be printed in the bulletin or available from pew Bibles.

A large church in Los Angeles had four ministries worshiping in the building: Filipino, Korean, Hispanic, and a mixed European American/African American congregation whose services were in

English. Several times a year they would join together for a multicultural worship service. The bulletin was printed on large paper with two columns on the left side of the bulletin and two columns on the right. Each column was a different language: Tagalog, Korean, Spanish, and English. There was truly a cacophony of voices, but people could participate throughout the worship service in their native languages.

Each of these models allows persons to worship in the language that is most comfortable for them. It can be seen as a form of access and hospitality.

Learning the Language of Another. Another approach to bilingual or multilingual culturally-conscious worship pushes everyone to learn the languages of the other cultures represented in the worship service. This does not mean that everyone is going to be fluent in all the languages represented but that the members might learn certain words, phrases, or songs that are common in the life of the multicultural community.

In this model, rather than allowing persons to worship exclusively in their native language (as in the fourth model), everyone is encouraged to sing in Spanish, Zulu, Tagalog, or Navaho. Members of various cultures may teach the congregation "The Peace of God be with You" in their native languages. The congregation may learn the Lord's Prayer or the Doxology in another language. At one time, a deaf member of the Dumbarton United Methodist Church taught the congregation how to "sing" the Doxology in sign language. This model is often more appropriate for the congregations whose dominant language is English. Those who are fully bilingual (fluent in two languages) may feel comfortable in either language. But those who struggle with English as a second language usually have the full burden of worshiping in a foreign tongue. They have to be bilingual to a certain degree to survive in this country. It is important that those of us for whom English is a first (and often only) language attempt to understand what being bilingual or multilingual means and how learning another's language (even if it is minimally) can make a person feel welcomed.

Summary

Your congregation may not fit exactly into any of these models. It may be a combination of two or more of the models listed above. Or you may be totally unique in the way you design worship for a multicultural congregation. While each of these models has limitations, each can also facilitate meaningful culturally-conscious worship. I cannot stress enough that much depends on the sensitivities and leadership of the pastor(s). Each multicultural congregation is unique. As Charles Foster suggests in *We Are the Church Together:*

> The task persons in these communities face is *not* that of becoming bilingual or multilingual or multicultural in the sense of mastering the multiple languages and cultures in currency. Rather, their task is to *appreciate* and *live in* rather than *master* or *resolve* the multiplicity of languages and cultures among them. Life in these communities calls persons toward the perception that experience can and should be interpreted and named in various ways, that truth can and should be viewed from differing angles simultaneously.[3]

One of these "viewing angles" is that of the Bible. It is important that all pastors who minister in multicultural congregations be rooted in biblical and theological visions for living out the Kingdom of God in a multicultural community. In many congregations, these biblical images and a theological language are the centerpoint around which the worship evolves. It is to that topic that I now turn.

---

[3]Charles R. Foster, *We Are the Church Together: Cultural Diversity in Congregational Life* (Valley Forge, Pa.: Trinity Press International, 1996), 158.

CHAPTER TWO

Kin-dom Visions and Kinship Values

Biblical and theological foundations are crucial to support culturally-conscious worship and the various ministries of multicultural congregations. While this is important for all congregations of whatever cultural heritage, it is even more important for multicultural congregations because the society in which we live reinforces the separation of races and cultures. A common story or vision rooted in the Christian faith is important as a cornerstone for our lives together.

Kin-dom Visions

As Christians, the very beginning of the church, what we call the "birthday" of the church, the Day of Pentecost, should be a clear sign to us of one of God's multicultural visions for the church. I am calling these visions God has for us "kin-dom visions" (using the term coined by Ada Maria Isasi-Diaz—*kin-dom*).[1] "Kin-dom" is reminiscent of all the images connected to the traditional phrase "kingdom of God," but "kin-dom" does not have the hierarchical implications, class divisions, and connotations of dominance and power associated with "kingdom." It also offers us a reminder that we are all kin—members of the family of God.

---

[1]Ada Maria Isasi-Diaz, "Solidarity: Love of Neighbor in the 1980s," in Susan Brooks Thistlethwaite and Mary Potter Engel, eds., *Lift Every Voice: Constructing Christian Theologies from the Underside* (San Francisco: Harper, 1990), 31–40.

The Day of Pentecost, then, is a vision of God's "kin-dom," a vision of mutuality and blessing, understanding one another's languages, joining together across racial, ethnic, and cultural boundaries. The Day of Pentecost is about God's making this multicultural mass of people into "kin"–brothers and sisters in the family of God. It's a wonderful, but very radical, proclamation of true community. What a great multicultural beginning of what we call the church! Given these beginnings of the Christian church, one could say that for the church to authentically be the "Church," we must be consciously seeking to live out this "kin-dom vision."

Acts 2

The story of Pentecost is not about speaking in tongues that no one could understand or that required a blessing upon another for the gift of interpreting that tongue. It is about bilingualism and multilingualism. It's about Jewish people from various cultures, ethnicities, and languages who gathered in one place–Jerusalem. Through the power of the Holy Spirit, the Jewish Christians from Galilee (those who had the message of Jesus) "began to speak in other languages, as the Spirit gave them ability" (Acts 2:4).

> And at this sound the crowd gathered and was bewildered, because each one heard them speaking in the native language of each. Amazed and astonished, they asked, "Are not all these who are speaking Galileans? And how is it that we hear, each of us, in our own native language? Parthians, Medes, Elamites, and residents of Mesopotamia, Judea and Cappadocia, Pontus and Asia, Phrygia and Pamphylia, Egypt and the parts of Libya belonging to Cyrene, and visitors from Rome...and Arabs–in our own languages we hear them speaking about God's deeds of power." (vv. 6–11)

Each heard in her or his own native language! In the United States today, the biblical Parthians and Medes are persons from Turkey who have immigrated here. They join the Mexican Americans and Vietnamese Americans, American citizens who have recently arrived from Africa and African Americans who have been on this soil for many generations, Native Americans who were here before the Europeans arrived, Koreans and Chinese and Japanese, Pacific Islanders and Caribbean Islanders.

The cultural diversity present in the church and society today is too great to list. Unfortunately, we are also often segregated from one another. But the birthday of the church is a celebration of the multicultural makeup of the early Christian community, a community not segregated from one another, but able to communicate with one another. The Pentecost story has been referred to as a "language miracle,"[2] and many of us wish it were that easy today. Unfortunately, learning another's language can be difficult and time consuming even with the help of the Holy Spirit. But it is not impossible. Many in our country today are not only bilingual but also multilingual. The experience of Pentecost lifts up for us a vision, a goal of being able to speak about the wondrous acts of God in languages that persons from other cultures can understand.

This text, however, is not just about multiethnic, multicultural, or multilingual issues. Peter also quotes Joel in verses 17 and 18:

> In the last days it will be, God declares, that I will pour out my Spirit upon all flesh, and your sons and your daughters shall prophesy, and your young men shall see visions, and your old men shall dream dreams. Even upon my slaves, both men and women, in those days I will pour out my Spirit; and they shall prophesy.

God's spirit falls on teenagers as well as retired folk, on women as well as men, and on those receiving welfare or those earning minimum wage as well as the middle and upper classes of society. Too often children, teenagers, and those in the last decades of their lives are often overlooked or ignored when it comes to the prophetic task of the church. This is true of women and the economically powerless as well. Yet the Pentecost story places these folk at the center as prophets of God.

Some use this text to argue that it's about missionary work alone—converting those who don't believe and then sending them back to their homogenous communities to live out the faith. And it's true that evangelism was taking place here. Verse 41 says, "So those who welcomed [Peter's] message were baptized, and that day about three thousand persons were added." But read on. Verses 42–47 say:

> They devoted themselves to the apostles' teaching and fellowship, to the breaking of bread and the prayers. Awe came upon everyone, because many wonders and signs were being done by the apostles. All who believed were together

---

[2]C. K. Barrett, *Acts,* vol. 1, The International Critical Commentary (Edinburgh: T. & T. Clark, 1994), 110; and Gerd Ludemann, *Early Christianity According to the Traditions in Acts: A Commentary* (Minneapolis: Fortress Press, 1987), 39.

and had all things in common; they would sell their possessions and goods and distribute the proceeds to all, as any had need. Day by day, as they spent much time together in the temple, they broke bread at home [or from house to house] and ate their food with glad and generous hearts, praising God and having the goodwill of all the people.

Some scholars say that these verses present Luke's ideal or his "utopian vision of what the church might be in its finest realization."[3] But even when Acts 2:42–47 is posited as an ideal, most agree that it is based on some reality. It is clear that the new converts learned from the teaching of the apostles, ate both daily meals and the unique Christian meal (the eucharist) with one another, and had fellowship with one another.

"Having all things in common" poses questions for some about the reality and feasibility of this for the early Christians. This phrase may well have been borrowed from a widespread Hellenistic axiom or proverb that says, "Friends hold all things in common." This proverb was one of the "most admired practices of antiquity"[4] and a hallmark of utopian visions of society.[5] "Communal possessions were not a goal of Rabbinical Judaism but the community at Qumran did have a strict rule of community possessions. Theirs was not based in friendship but was rooted in a strict rule of ritual purity."[6]

Sharing one's possessions was a requirement if one wanted to join the Qumran community (similar to later monastic orders). For Luke, however, "having all things in common" was presented as a "spontaneous outgrowth of the Spirit" rather than as an ideal of friendship or institutional rule for community membership.[7]

Nothing is said in Acts about a *law* requiring converts to the Christian Church to hand over their property, and other differences distinguish the church as described in Acts from the Essenes and from the Qumran sect. It is undoubtedly true and important that at the time of Christian origins various forms of communal rather than private ownership of wealth were being practised, and it is quite reasonable to conclude that the Christians followed a similar plan.[8]

---

[3]Luke Timothy Johnson, *The Acts of the Apostles,* Sacra Pagina (Collegeville, Minn.: Liturgical Press, 1992), 63; and Barrett, *Acts,* 162.
[4]Barrett, *Acts,* 168.
[5]Johnson, *Acts,* 58.
[6]Ibid., 59.
[7]Ibid.
[8]Barrett, *Acts,* 168.

For most Christians today, "having all things in common" is more an ideal or kin-dom vision than reality. Nonetheless, the four common practices of this early Christian community are important for multicultural congregations today.

1. *Learning from the Apostles.* Studying biblical texts together and discerning present-day apostles and prophets can build up the body of Christ and impart wisdom to the various members.
2. *Fellowship.* While fellowship in verses 42–47 is broadly defined, it refers to communal activities as well as almsgiving and the sharing of possessions. Contributing our presence to the community as well as our resources will enhance the well-being of individuals and the community as a whole.
3. *Breaking Bread Together.* Participation in the Christian meal of holy communion as well as sharing meals with one another at the church or in various homes bonds persons from diverse cultures into a family–the family of God.
4. *Praising God.* Praising God is at the core of Jewish and Christian worship. At the beginning of the church, persons from different cultures worshiped together. It is the joy of multicultural congregations that it is happening again today!

The story of Pentecost is about a multicultural, multiethnic, multiclass, intergenerational community that, to some degree, held things in common, spent time together in the temple, ate together, broke bread in various homes, and praised God–they worshiped together. They had the goodwill of *all* the people. The second chapter of the book of Acts is a rich vision of what God's will for the church could or should be. It is filled with images that can truly sustain a multicultural community that takes native languages, gender issues, class issues, and justice issues seriously.

Peter's Conversion

Those who came to know Jesus at Pentecost were Jews who were present in Jerusalem to celebrate *Shavuoth,* the Jewish Feast of Weeks. They came from various cultures, but they shared the Jewish story of salvation history. They accepted Jesus as the long-awaited Messiah. Accepting Gentiles, however, was a different story. Peter and Paul and many of the other disciples were so acculturated in the laws of Judaism that it was difficult for them to discern God's vision for the Gentiles. Segregation was a strong cultural and religious value; Jews didn't eat or associate with Gentiles. Acts 10 and 11, however, describe

Peter's conversion on this topic. At the beginning of Acts 10, a Gentile centurion named Cornelius has a dream where God tells him to send for Peter. The next day, God sends a vision to Peter. In this vision,

> [Peter] saw the heaven opened and something like a large sheet coming down, being lowered to the ground by its four corners. In it were all kinds of four-footed creatures and reptiles and birds of the air. Then he heard a voice saying, "Get up, Peter; kill and eat." But Peter said, "By no means, Lord; for I have never eaten anything that is profane or unclean." The voice said to him again, a second time, "What God has made clean, you must not call profane." This happened three times, and the thing was suddenly taken up to heaven. (10:11–16)

This section in Acts is about Peter's growing awareness that *profane* and *unclean* are human terms that establish barriers between persons seeking God. He is converted by a kin-dom vision from God to believe that "what God has made clean, you must not call profane" (10:15b and 11:9) "The Spirit told me...not to make a distinction between them [Gentiles] and us" (11:12a).

Later in chapter 10, Peter said to them, "You yourselves know that it is unlawful for a Jew to associate with or to visit a Gentile; but God has shown me that I should not call anyone profane or unclean" (v. 28).

It's not that Peter was totally opposed to Gentiles becoming believers in Jesus. But prior to his kin-dom vision, Peter believed the Gentiles must first become Jews; they must become assimilated into the Jewish religion (including circumcision for the men) before they could become rightful heirs of God. But after the kin-dom vision, Peter changed his mind: "I truly understand that God shows no partiality, but in every nation anyone who fears him and does what is right is acceptable to him" (10:34–35).

In chapter 11, "the circumcised believers criticized [Peter]" (v. 2) for eating with uncircumcised men and for believing that they received the Holy Spirit. But after Peter explains to them his vision from God, they, too, change their minds and begin to live into this kin-dom vision. Peter says to them, "If then God gave them [the Gentiles] the same gift that [God] gave us when we believed in the Lord Jesus Christ, who was I that I could hinder God?" (v. 17). When those who chastised Peter heard this, "they were silenced. And they praised God, saying, 'Then God has given even to the Gentiles the repentance that leads to life'" (v. 18).

Our culture likewise values segregation of religions and ethnicities. Too often our own language explicitly or implicitly names those different from us as "unclean" or "profane"—as not as good as we are or not as worthy of God's attention and love. Here in Acts, Peter recognizes his own ethnocentrism and offers us God's kin-dom vision for living in a diverse community, a kin-dom vision of God's unconditional love for all.

Paul's Conversion

Paul's announcement of his decision to take the good news of Jesus to the Gentiles comes after a long sermon in the synagogue that recounts Israel's salvation history and the death and resurrection of Jesus. He is a devout Jew preaching to Jews to convince them to accept Jesus. And Acts 13:42–44 suggests that many received his message and wanted to hear more.

> When the meeting of the synagogue broke up, many Jews and devout converts to Judaism followed Paul and Barnabas, who spoke to them and urged them to continue in the grace of God. The next sabbath almost the whole city gathered to hear the word of the Lord.

But as is often the case, there were some who became jealous at the number of people who had gathered to hear Paul. In response to their resistance and rejection, "Paul and Barnabas spoke out boldly, saying, 'It was necessary that the word of God should be spoken first to you. Since you reject it and judge yourselves to be unworthy of eternal life, we are now turning to the Gentiles'" (13:46).

In many ways, this is reminiscent of the European American church today. We preach to "our own kind" but many don't appear to be listening. Christians from other cultures, however, are growing in numbers on this soil and all over the globe.

Peter's and Paul's conversion to accepting Gentiles as full Christians, however, was not sufficient. The controversy continued among the apostles and elders in Jerusalem. Acts 15:5 says, "But some believers who belonged to the sect of the Pharisees stood up and said, 'It is necessary for them to be circumcised and ordered to keep the law of Moses.'"

But after Paul testified to the "signs and wonders that God had done through them among the Gentiles" (v. 12), James, speaking on behalf of the apostles and elders in Jerusalem, supported the work among the Gentiles and said,

> Therefore I have reached a decision that we should not
> trouble those Gentiles who are turning to God, but we should
> write to them to abstain only from things polluted by idols
> and from fornication and from whatever has been strangled
> and from blood. (vv. 19–20)

A compromise was reached and the mission to the Gentiles seemed to be in full swing.

Paul wanted *everyone* to have access to the saving grace of Jesus, not just Jews. And the theology Paul developed through his writing has had lasting influence on the church. Paul's theology includes several aspects. "For the sake of equality Paul discards genealogy."[9] No more is birth into a particular people the sign of being chosen by God. Instead, anyone who has faith in Christ inherits the promises of God. Theologian Miroslav Volf states that "Paul deprived each culture of ultimacy in order to give them all legitimacy in the wider family of cultures."[10]

Paul's theology also included the idea that we are not individual bodies who are united somehow by a greater universal spirit, but rather that we are a "community of interrelated bodies" who form the body of Christ.[11] We are one body with many members, and when one member rejoices, we all rejoice, and when one suffers, we all suffer. "For in the one Spirit we were all baptized into one body—Jews or Greeks, slaves or free—and we were all made to drink of one Spirit" (1 Cor. 12:13).

We are interconnected one to the other across race, ethnicity, class, and gender lines. One's genealogy or the status of one's parents is no longer important. No matter who we are, as Christians we are kin to one another in the body of Christ.

Multiethnic Heritage

The multiethnic heritage of the biblical story gives mixed messages concerning intermarriage and the children of these unions. On the one hand, in the book of Jeremiah, it is written:

> Thus says the LORD of hosts, the God of Israel, to all the
> exiles whom I have sent into exile from Jerusalem to Babylon:
> Build houses and live in them; plant gardens and eat what

---

[9]Miroslav Volf, *Exclusion and Embrace: A Theological Exploration of Identity, Otherness, and Reconciliation* (Nashville: Abingdon Press, 1996), 34.

[10]Ibid., 49.

[11]Ibid., 48.

they produce. Take wives and have sons and daughters; take wives for your sons, and give your daughters in marriage, that they may bear sons and daughters; multiply there, and do not decrease. But seek the welfare of the city where I have sent you into exile, and pray to the LORD on its behalf, for in its welfare you will find your welfare. (Jer. 29:4–7)

On the other hand, upon the peoples' return from exile to Jerusalem, the book of Ezra says,

"The land that you are entering to possess is a land unclean with the pollutions of the peoples of the lands, with their abominations. They have filled it from end to end with their uncleanness. Therefore do not give your daughters to their sons, neither take their daughters for your sons, and never seek their peace or prosperity, so that you may be strong and eat the good of the land and leave it for an inheritance to your children forever." After all that has come upon us for our evil deeds and for our great guilt, seeing that you, our God, have punished us less than our iniquities deserved and have given us such a remnant as this, shall we break your commandments again and intermarry with the peoples who practice these abominations? (9:11b–14)

Keep in mind however, that this admonition in Ezra (similar to the one in Deuteronomy 7:3–4a when the Hebrew people first entered the promised land) is concerned with *religious* purity rather than racial/cultural purity. In Ezra the people who stayed behind in Jerusalem (while others were carted off into exile) began to lose their faith. They intermarried but also began to adopt some of the gods worshiped among the other people.[12] Keeping the Jewish faith unpolluted by pagan gods was important—especially as the exiles reentered the promised land.

Before and after Ezra, however, some people of faith intermarried. Biracial or multicultural families are not a recent development (neither are interfaith marriages). Moses married Zipporah, who was a Midianite (Ex. 2:21). Their children were biethnic, bicultural, and possibly bilingual.

---

[12]F. Charles Fensham, *The Books of Ezra and Nehemiah* (Grand Rapids, Mich.: Eerdmans, 1982), 124.

Ruth, the Moabite, was not raised Jewish, but after the death of her husband, she went back to live with Naomi's people, to follow Naomi's God. Her children were the result of the union between her and Boaz. Their children were likewise biethnic, bicultural, and possibly bilingual. Solomon was born to David and Bathsheba, who was presumably a Hittite (her first husband Uriah was a Hittite).

Today, interfaith marriages and intermarriage by Christians from different ethnic cultures can be fraught with tension. In some Asian cultures, this is referred to as "out-marrying"—marrying outside one's culture. Some Christians follow the advice attributed to God in Jeremiah and settle down in their new homeland and marry without regard to ethnicity. Others follow the admonition attributed to God in the book of Ezra and marry within their cultural group.

For those who have intermarried and have had children who are biracial or multiethnic, it's important that they can find their story in God's story of salvation history. These children often feel isolated in our society because they are not totally accepted by either culture/race. For biracial and multiethnic persons in our society, there is a rich resource wherein to find their own story in the story of these important people of faith. Many multicultural congregations have some members who are in mixed marriages with biracial children. They belong in the Christian community and should find a welcome there.

Early Christian Community

The political and social environment of the early Christian community in Greco-Roman times was truly multicultural, multiethnic, and multireligious. It was not unlike what we are experiencing today. In his chapter "Clashing Cultures," New Testament scholar Burton Mack describes the issues at hand for the early church:

> Not only were peoples of all ethnic extractions living together in cities without a common culture, the histories of incessant warring and rapid political changeovers settled into convoluted layers of bitter memories and hatreds.[13]

> ...Beneath the surface, serious cultural conflict swirled around such issues as homosexuality (a moral problem for Jews but not for Greeks); prostitution (accepted by the Greeks as a

_____

[13]Burton Mack, *Who Wrote the New Testament?* (San Francisco: Harper San Francisco, 1995), 26.

fact of city life but regarded by the Jews as threatening family values); the laws that governed marriage, divorce, and the treatment of slaves; the cultural and cultic significance of foods and family meals; the public role of women, proper attire; and attendance at the baths, athletic events, banquets, civic feasts ("sacrifices"), and festivals. Differences in codes of purity, propriety, ranking, honor, and shame created friction for people of diverse cultural and ethnic backgrounds.[14]

And in the midst of this confusion, Jesus' message offered a unifying religious and social vision—the kin-dom of God. He called people to an alternative way of life that was available for anyone—regardless of race, ethnicity, gender, or class. This lifestyle called for change—sometimes radical change in behavior and belief—yet it promised love, belonging, and justice in this world and eternal life in the world to come.[15]

This vision captured the imaginations and souls of many persons from diverse ethnic, cultural, and religious backgrounds. We know that many of these diverse people worshiped together, but we don't have biblical records that are clear on the content of their worship practices. We do know that Jewish worship traditions (reading of scripture, commentary on the text/preaching) greatly influenced Christian worship patterns, that the Greco-Roman banquet patterns had an impact on the Christian common meal,[16] and that elements of the mystery religions also influenced the liturgy.[17] Today scholars are beginning to show the influence of the Greek classics (e.g., *Iliad* and *Odyssey*) on Christianity.[18] Mack states, "Christianity drew now upon some Jewish roots, now upon Greek ideas, and eventually became infatuated with the idea of Roman power."[19]

We also know that the earliest Christian communities had tremendous diversity in their worship practices. While there have been attempts throughout Christian history to unify the liturgy so

---

[14]Ibid., 27.

[15]Ibid., 40.

[16]Dennis E. Smith and Hal E. Taussig, *Many Tables: The Eucharist in the New Testament and Liturgy Today* (Philadelphia: Trinity Press International, 1990), 21–35.

[17]Gregory Riley, *One Jesus, Many Christs* (San Francisco: Harper San Francisco, 1997), 149. See also "The Mysteries within Judaism and Christianity," in Marvin W. Meyer, *The Ancient Mysteries* (San Francisco: Harper & Row, 1987).

[18]Dennis MacDonald, *The Homeric Epics and the Gospel of Mark* (New Haven, Conn.: Yale University Press, 2000).

[19]Mack, *Who Wrote the New Testament?* 41.

that all Christian worship was the same, these attempts have always met with resistance. Today we have a diversity of denominations within the Christian church—each with its own worship style, form, and content. Even within the Roman Catholic Church, the cultural diversity of its members has greatly influenced the "look" and "feel" of the worship services in any particular parish.

While attempts at unifying the liturgy have never fully succeeded, segregation of persons according to their ethnicity and culture became more and more acceptable until it was viewed as the norm. In many ways, cultural or kinship values won out over the kin-dom vision. We have strayed far from our beginnings on that day of Pentecost. Multicultural congregations and culturally-conscious worship are attempts at reclaiming that kin-dom vision despite our ethnocentric instincts to segregate into groups of like kin.

Kinship Values

While *kin-dom visions* denotes a community of diverse people living a life of fellowship, mutuality, and solidarity, *kinship values* refers to both the unique aspects of every culture and the extreme attitudes that reject anyone who is not of the same ethnicity, clan, or tribe. Kinship values are those attitudes inherent in all cultures that cause us to value those like us more than those who seem different. In times of crisis or chaos, these kinship values cause us to "take care of our own." In times of uncertainty, the "other" is blamed for all the problems (lack of jobs, crime, social instability, etc.) experienced in society and in one's own family.

Unfortunately, there is much in our society and in our individual cultural backgrounds that leads to separation, segregation, and divisiveness. It is easy to articulate God's kin-dom vision, but much harder to live it out. There are many things that stand in our way— economics, historical backgrounds, and individual personalities. I want to focus, however, on our various ethnocentric attitudes or kinship values and how we approach cultural diversity.

In the Greco-Roman world, the cultures that collided all had their own stories about how the world was created, and each established their worldview and cultural values as the universal norm. "Every people of antiquity had imagined themselves at the center of a vast universe that had been created just for them, with a special place for them to construct their kind of society."[20]

---

[20]Ibid., 29.

Today we might have a broader perspective on the interrelatedness of this global community of ours, but many cultures still see their values and ways of perceiving the world as the most natural, the best fit with the universe. We want God to be on the side of our particular culture. We sing "God Bless America." The British sing "God Save the Queen." And British and American imperialism have impacted the world in economics, English-language preference, and Christian superiority through missionary zeal.

Extreme forms of ethnocentrism also affect us today. The Nazis claimed that God was on the side of Protestant Christians, and all those "others"–particularly the Jews–were expendable. Ethnic cleansing, hate crimes, and holy wars are all about claiming a particular cultural and/or religious superiority. God loves "us" and despises "you," therefore "you"–the other–must become like us or be excluded, or even eliminated, in some way.

Conversations about "difference" and "cultural diversity" abound in our society today. In politics, one question is how a democratic society can live up to its ideal of "all persons are created equal?" What does this mean for issues of affirmative action, bilingual education, and preservation of the land and water rights of Native Americans? If all persons are equal, should some get preferential treatment? Clearly "equality for all" has been and still is an ideal. What about righting past wrongs and balancing unequal treatment in the past to create a more level playing field for today?

In the field of education, how does one respect the various cultural differences among the students in the classroom? What effect does cultural diversity have on curriculum design, textbook choice, and teacher training? How much can we expect teachers to learn? to teach? How much can we expect students to learn? Who establishes the priorities about what will and will not be taught? What constitutes a safe and empowering educational environment for students of various cultures?

In the area of social psychology, how do persons come to understand themselves as creatures of culture? What stages do persons go through in determining their own complex cultural identities? How do persons deal with the cultural identity of the other?…embrace the other?…recognize the other as different?…recognize the other as the same?…ignore those who are different?…reject those who are different?…or resort to violence or hate crimes to exclude the other?

In the field of law, what constitutes an illegal alien, an undocumented worker, and all the other legal terminology used to identify persons who are not United States citizens? What roles do ethnicity and culture play in the laws determining who can stay in this country and who will be deported? Is "equality for all" merely a legal term meaning we are all equal under the law (or at least all United States citizens are equal under the law)? Is the concept "equality for all" more ambiguous in terms of education, health care, and those who are not here "legally"?

What is our goal as Christians in regard to diversity? Converting everyone to be like us—culturally and religiously? Tolerance of difference? Working toward a "color-blind" church and society? Honoring and celebrating diversity?

All these issues should be important in the lives of all Christian congregations, but certainly in multicultural congregations. How do Christians respond to these diverse and complex issues? There are no easy answers, but the multicultural church has a unique opportunity to provide leadership in these other "secular" arenas. Multicultural congregations know something about creating communities that live with real differences, that live well and thrive on diversity.

This next section explores the ethnocentric perspectives that exclude others (explicitly and implicitly) and the importance of recognizing the unique personhood of the other. Where we are in terms of our own identity development, how we individually and collectively as a faith community approach the reality of "difference," and what it means to live multiculturally will also be discussed.

Forms of Exclusion

There are many ways in which persons exclude others.[21] The most extreme is a fear or hatred so great that one seeks to eliminate the other. History has given us many examples of holy wars and ethnic wars where violence and murder are justified in the name of religious or cultural superiority. It is what happened to the Jews in the Nazi death camps, what happened to those in Rwanda, Bosnia, and Kosovo. But we also see this form of exclusion on a much smaller scale in the hate crimes perpetuated in this country. Someone believes in the superiority of his or her race, culture, religious belief, or moral stance and targets those who represent their hatred of the other: tying an African American teenaged boy to the bumper of a car and dragging him behind the moving car until he is dead; opening fire on a Jewish community center; bombing abortion clinics; tying a young gay man to a fence and beating him to death. It would be nice to

---

[21]Volf, *Exclusion and Embrace,* 75–76, identifies three forms of exclusion: (1) elimination, (2) assimilation, (3) abandonment.

place this extreme form of exclusion outside the realm of Christian behavior, but we know too well that Christians are not exempt from violence in the name of religion, race, and morality.

There are more subtle forms of exclusion, however, that many of us participate in. Assimilationism is another way we exclude the essence of the other by forcing them to become like us. It requires the other to adopt the values, worldview, customs, and ritual practices of the dominant group. A person is in many ways asked to give up the past, his or her cultural norms and identity, in order to be accepted by those in power.

One can also be excluded by being ignored, being made invisible. We often ignore the cleaning people or mail clerks, the street cleaners, the gardeners, or the homeless begging for assistance. We ignore children and the elderly, persons who live with mental and physical disabilities, and many who appear to be "different." Sometimes we ignore out of ignorance, sometimes out of fear, sometimes out of embarrassment or feeling uncomfortable, sometimes just because we are shy or don't know what to say to one another. But ignoring persons is a form of exclusion. When I was in deaf ministry, hearing persons would often use me as an interpreter to convey a message to a deaf person. The hearing person, however, would often look at me and totally ignore the deaf person who was the intended receiver of the message. The deaf persons would get so frustrated, even angry, at such behavior, which excluded them. Who in your environment is often ignored? In committee meetings or fellowship activities, take notice of who is left alone and ignored.

Those in multicultural congregations have in many ways moved along the continuum toward a greater respect for diversity. Nonetheless, various forms of exclusion can still persist. Some multicultural congregations may prefer to accept only persons from other cultures who have a fluency in the English language because bilingual worship and ministry requires so much extra time, energy, and financial resources. Beyond worship, the "power" positions in the church may still be held by persons of the majority culture in the congregation, except for a token representative here or there. The message sent is that "You may join us, but we are still in control."

Symbolic forms of exclusion take place on a regular basis.[22] Someone may tell an ethnic joke or make a sexist comment. A flight of stairs leading up to the entrance of the church is a clear, often

---

[22]Ibid.

unintentional, but symbolic, statement that persons who cannot walk or climb stairs are not welcome.

We also exclude and demean others by the language we use. Constantly associating the word *black* with darkness and evil, and *white* with goodness and purity symbolically excludes persons whose skin color is *black* from participation in the holy realm of God. Referring to *blindness* or *deafness* only in negative terms referring to the sin of disobedience or a willful break in one's relationship with God excludes persons who are physically blind or deaf from faithful obedience to God. Language such as "mankind" or the generic "he" excludes women from humanity. Language that claims God is only male symbolically excludes women from being made in the image of God.

There is additional language that excludes the other. Use of language that identifies the other as lazy, a parasite, a fag, mentally retarded, illiterate, an illegal alien, or someone who can't speak English allows us to justify our own inhuman actions that exclude the other. If we can identify people as morally, intellectually, or physically inferior or "abnormal" (based on our definition of "normal"), it is easier for us to rationalize our exclusion of their presence among us.

Symbolic forms of exclusion are necessary to develop the kind of superiority and hatred that often lead to more extreme forms of hatred and violence. Our ethnocentric attitudes and kinship values often exclude the other. But more importantly, they also prevent us from attaining the kin-dom visions given to us in the Bible.

Stages of Cultural Identity

My nephew Jeremy has a father from Mexico and a European American mother who is a deaf-education teacher and teaches in sign language. When Jeremy was about three and a half, he figured out that everything in his world had three "names": an English name, a Spanish name, and a sign name. I'd take him to the park and he'd want to know the three "names" for everything–the tree, rocks, swings, clouds, dog, and so on. One day when he was about four years old, I took him to a Korean dinner at the seminary. He was outside playing with the other children. After a while, he came in and said, "The kids are speaking Spanish." I said, "No, they're speaking Korean. It's a different language than Spanish or English." You could see his mind working overtime. Suddenly his eyes got big and he slapped his cheeks with the palms of his hands and shouted, "Not four!?!?" It was a statement and a question. It suddenly dawned on him that his world was bigger than he had thought. He realized that there were four words for everything instead of three. When I tried to explain to him that my deaf friend who was visiting from Korea used a Korean sign language that was different from the sign language he was learning and that his baby-sitter spoke Tongan, it was a little too much for him to take. He's only five now, but already he has a larger grasp of the world than I did when I was in high school growing up in an all-white town where foreign languages were something you studied in school but that had no experiential connection to individuals or communities of persons.

When most of us develop a sense of our own cultural identities, it is usually in response to surface kinds of cultural differences: skin color, languages, foods people eat, clothes people wear, musical instruments they play. For many people, it takes much longer to understand that few things in this world are culturally neutral or culture-free. Coming to terms with one's own cultural identity and the cultural identity of others is a process. Some studies have been done to ascertain the stages people go through in their cultural identity development and their relationships to persons of other cultures.[23] These stages differ depending on whether one is from the majority culture or a minority one.

These stages are generalized, and not everyone passes through all of the stages. For some, the developmental process is halted in a particular stage. For everyone, much depends on one's environment growing up–not just one's physical environment but the attitudinal

---

[23]C. W. Thomas, *Boys No More* (Beverly Hills: Glencoe Press, 1971), identifies five stages for black persons' experience at varying degrees: (1) Persons experience some confusion about their black identity and look to the dominant society for self-definition. To move beyond this, one must *withdraw* to come to a clearer understanding of oneself. (2) One must then *testify* to the pain previously experienced in denying oneself as a person. (3) Then seek out and *process information* about racism and one's cultural heritage. (4) *Actively work* to find a connection to the larger black experience. (5) The *transcendental* stage is where the person loses any previously held hang-ups about social class and race and sees oneself as a part of humanity in all its forms.

W. E. Cross in "The Negro-to-Black Conversion Experience: Toward a Psychology of Black Liberation" *Black World* 20 (1971): 13–27, identifies four stages: (1) pre-encounter, (2) encounter, (3) immersion, and (4) internalization.

Helms in "Toward a Theoretical Explanation of the Effects of Race on Counseling: A Black and White Model," *The Counseling Psychologist* 12 (1985): 153–65, identifies five stages for persons of the majority culture: (1) contact, (2) disintegration, (3) reintegration, (4) pseudo-independence, and (5) autonomy.

Joseph Ponterotto in "Racial Consciousness Development Among White Counselor Trainees," *Journal of Multicultural Counseling and Development* 16 (October 1988): 146–56, identifies four stages for persons of the majority culture: (1) pre-exposure, (2) exposure, (3) zealot-defensive, and (4) integration.

environment of one's parents, extended family, and influential community. At one end of the spectrum are those who are raised to be blatantly racist. They start out in an anger stage with hostility toward those of other races and cultures and take on the responsibility to defend their own culture (even to the point of violence). At the other end of the spectrum are those who grow up in multicultural environments, being encouraged to make friends with persons of other cultures, to learn some of their languages, to eat their food, and to share in their cultural holidays and rituals. Some go through these stages early in life and others much later. While there are many variables for both those of the majority culture and those of minority cultures, some general observations can be made.

Identity Development of Persons from Minority Cultures

Keep in mind that depending on the important influences in one's upbringing, one may begin at any stage. The range of stages for persons from minority cultures approximates the following:

1. Many persons from minority cultures at one point or another accept the majority culture's attitude toward them. They come to believe what the dominant culture says about them. They internalize the second-class citizen status projected upon them by the majority culture. Eventually, they may believe that the European American race and culture are superior, and that their race and culture are inferior. This is especially true of recent immigrants from poorer countries who see America as the "promised land" in terms of economics and education. This can also be found, however, among women who have accepted the dominant gender's attitude toward them and have internalized the second-class status projected upon females in our male-dominated culture.

2. Over time, they come to realize that the European American culture is not so great. They begin to label experiences of racism, oppression, and unfair treatment. They realize that they have begun to lose the ties to their own cultural identities and historical roots. They start to see that buying into the dominant culture's definition of them works against them as individuals and as a collective group. They come to understand the effect that racism (or patriarchy) has on their sense of self, their self-worth and self-esteem, and how they have

participated in it by believing the propaganda of the dominant culture. They begin to rebel.

3. This rebellion can manifest itself in anger and hostility toward the dominant culture. It can also result in an exclusive identification with one's own culture. We saw this in the black power movement of the 1970s. We experienced this in the early feminist movement and are still living with some of the fallout of that period where people today see all feminists as "man-haters" and separatists. When I was working as a chaplain at Gallaudet University (a college for deaf students in Washington, D.C.), there were always several deaf students raised in hearing families who believed themselves to be inferior to hearing persons. When they reached stage two and came to realize the richness of the deaf culture and their oppression by the hearing society, their anger and hostility toward hearing people grew. Many who wore hearing aids or could speechread (lipread) or even speak chose to take their hearing aids off and refused to speak. They wanted to exclusively identify and associate with the deaf world, and for them it meant communicating solely through sign language.

4. Those who move beyond stage three become comfortable in who they are. They honor and value their own culture and have found self-esteem as an individual and as a member of a particular cultural group. The anger dissipates and the hostility is resolved. They are better able to deal realistically with the majority culture and can move between both cultures.

5. Some move on to actively fight racism (or sexism or oralism) and to resolve tension between various cultural entities. They see learning about other cultures as an opportunity to learn more about themselves and the world in which they live.

6. Just because a person goes through these various stages, it doesn't mean that some experience won't take the person back to an earlier stage. Persons may come to terms with the majority culture but may someday be faced with tensions between their particular cultural group and another minority group. This can be seen among the African American community and Hispanics in Southern California or between some Koreans and African Americans, or between feminists and womanists. One must individually and collectively come to terms with one's cultural identity and status in relationship to these other cultural groups.

Identity Development of Persons from Majority Cultures

One's upbringing also influences greatly the cultural identity development of persons from the majority culture. Those raised in the Los Angeles basin will experience diversity much more quickly than those raised in a small Midwestern town composed almost solely of persons of European ancestry. These stages are very generalized, and, as with the development of persons from minority cultures, one may never move through all the stages.

1. In many predominantly European American communities, persons have often given little thought to multicultural issues, the meaning of cultural diversity in society, or one's role as a member of the dominant culture in a racist society. People know that diversity exists out there somewhere, but it receives little intellectual or emotional investment.

2. At some point in a person's life, one is exposed to cultural difference on a *relational* level and comes to realize the realities of racism and discrimination. A person may be racist but become friends with an African American woman at work. One response is, "But she's not like 'the rest of them.'" Or the person may be forced to examine the dominant culture's values that contribute to these oppressive attitudes and behaviors and one's role as a member of this dominant group. One may be against gays and lesbians, but when a good friend comes out as gay, the relationship challenges preconceived attitudes and beliefs.

3. With more exposure and understanding of cultural differences, one realizes the world is not culturally neutral, that politics, education, even worship, are culturally influenced. Objective truth may be challenged. One may become angry about racism and injustice, or one might feel guilty for consciously or unconsciously participating in the perpetuation of oppression toward persons of other cultures.

4. The consciousness raising of stage three and the awareness of a world that is not as certain as one originally thought can be very unsettling. It can cause excitement and curiosity in some and outright fear and defensiveness in others. At this stage, one often makes a decision to either side with the minority situation and learn more about cultural difference in its multivalent dimensions or retreat and retrench oneself in defending the privileged position of the dominant culture.

Those who side with the minority "plight" may take on an extreme (and often unhealthy) goal of "saving" those who have been oppressed from the evils of society. Some reject their own culture and try to immerse themselves in another culture. Many, however, develop strong analysis skills as well as relational skills and come to know the complexities involved and how to use one's power as a member of the dominant culture in empowering ways.

5. Over time, persons develop a more balanced approach to cultural diversity that involves a healthy curiosity about other cultures, an appreciation of cultural differences, and a true valuation and respect of persons from other cultures. One also comes to realize that all cultures are human developments and require critique. The greatest difficulty is defining the standard for cultural critique, for all standards are also culturally influenced. In the Christian church, we search our souls and our resources for a standard based in God's love and justice.

These stages are in many ways artificial, and yet they can help us examine our own lives in terms of the development of our own cultural identities. They can also help us articulate how our congregations see themselves along these various continuums.

Those of us who function in a minority culture and majority culture simultaneously may find ourselves in both of these models of cultural identity development. As a European American female, I experience some of the stages in the "minority" section as a female in a male-dominated society, but as a European American, I am a member of the majority culture. An African American male has power as a male in this culture but is perceived as a minority because of his African ancestry. A European American male who is gay or a European American male whose legs were amputated may be part of the dominant culture through ethnicity and gender but may be oppressed as a person who is gay or who lives with a disability.

Recognition and Misrecognition

It's an important part of all of our lives to be recognized as persons of worth, to know that by our very existence we belong to the human community. Our identities are shaped by how people "recognize" us, how they name who we are. Likewise, our identities can also be shaped by how we are not recognized or are *mis*recognized:

...our identity is partly shaped by recognition or its absence, often by the *mis*recognition of others, and so a person or group of people can suffer real damage, real distortion, if the people or society around them mirror back to them a confining or demeaning or contemptible picture of themselves. Nonrecognition or misrecognition can inflict harm, can be a form of oppression, imprisoning someone in a false, distorted, and reduced mode of being.[24]

When women argue for inclusive language, it is an attempt to be recognized as part of the human race. When persons with disabilities fought for the passage of the Americans with Disabilities Act, it was their way of forcing the country to recognize them as people (like everyone else) who want access to movie theaters and restaurants and churches.

The early constitution of the United States (Article 1, Section 3) *mis*recognized persons of African descent by stating that black men should only be counted as three-fifths of a "real" (i.e., white) man. That *mis*recognition continued for decades and still exists today in a variety of forms of discrimination and oppression. "Recognition is not just a courtesy we owe people. It is a vital human need."[25] Not recognizing the other or *mis*recognizing those who are different from us erects barriers to attaining kin-dom visions.

Recognizing the uniqueness of various cultural groups has received much attention in the past twenty years. There is a downfall, however. In our efforts to recognize cultural diversity, we may end up stereotyping individuals because of their skin color or ethnicity. We may assume that a person who "looks Japanese" would prefer a Japanese-speaking worship service, when in reality the person may be second- or third-generation American and not speak Japanese at all.

We might assume that a person who is "black" in skin tone is an African American and would prefer a particular type of music or preaching in worship. In reality, however, the person may be from Cuba and speak Spanish or be from Haiti and speak Creole or French and have totally different expectations in regard to music and preaching. Or the person may be African American but doesn't find the traditional black church worship style to be her or his liturgical homeland.

---

[24]Charles Taylor, *Multiculturalism: Examining the Politics of Recognition,* 2d ed. (Princeton, N.J.: Princeton University Press, 1994), 25.

[25] Ibid., 26.

Stereotyping also does a tremendous disservice to the increasingly biracial and multiethnic members of our society—many of whom are children. How do they possibly choose which group to identify with when in their very being they are a mixture of both? Stereotyping a person because of his or her skin color or ethnicity can limit a person's identity, range of interests, and relationships. Yet not recognizing or *mis*recognizing their unique cultural heritage, history, and ethnic ties can also deny an important part of who they are.

There can sometimes be a fine line between recognizing the uniqueness of the other and stereotyping the other. But it is important to attempt the one (recognition) without falling into the trap of the other (stereotyping).

Perspectives on Difference

In any multicultural context, it's important to understand how we ourselves view the notion of "difference." What is our individual view about those who are different, and what is the general perspective of our congregation about difference?[26]

1. ***Ethnocentric Approach.*** This is the typical attitude that my culture, my "race," my nation is superior to yours. The behavior of persons who hold this perspective may be to totally dismiss those who are different as inferior and therefore not worthy of their time or recognition, or they may become assimilationist by trying to make everyone else be just like them.

2. ***Ignore Difference.*** There are some people who choose to ignore difference. In many cases it is an attempt to say, "We are all the same," so differences are irrelevant. "Let's focus on our commonality and ignore the differences." For many persons, the goal of a "color-blind" society is very real. However, in reality, skin color, facial features, hair texture, ethnicity, nationality, language proficiency, physical and mental abilities, educational level, and economic level are often judged as not only different but also as "second class" in this society.

---

[26]Eric Law, *The Bush Was Blazing but Not Consumed* (St. Louis: Chalice Press, 1996), 47–60, identifies seven responses to difference: (1) Difference does not exist; (2) Difference is confined to broad categories; (3) You are different, therefore you are bad; (4) It's okay for you to be different, but I am better; (5) I am different; therefore I am bad and you are good; (6) If you don't include like I do, you are bad; and (7) I know there are differences, but they are not important.

Ignoring difference also strips persons of their uniqueness—their cultural, ethnic, and religious heritages. Some persons from minority cultures in this country experience this "ignoring of difference" as rendering them invisible to the rest of society and depriving them of their sense of cultural identity. Or they may perceive this "ignoring of difference" to imply that "You are just like me" (i.e., white), which is also not true, since on a group basis, persons of non-European ancestry don't receive the same treatment as European Americans in this culture.

3. ***Internalized Inferiority.*** This approach to difference presumes that the dominant culture is right—they are superior, and I am inferior. This attitude often comes from minority persons who have internalized the *mis*recognition given to them and have accepted the prevalent attitude that the dominant culture, language, and values are better than their own. But this attitude can also be found among persons of the majority culture who find their culture lacking in many ways. They immerse themselves in another culture because they find it to be richer in history, foods, language, traditional dance, cultural symbols, and rituals. While persons of the majority culture may identify the surface elements of their culture as inferior, they seldom internalize this attitude of inferiority for themselves as individual agents because the dominant society still treats them as "one of them."

4. ***Unity in Diversity.*** This approach to difference honors the uniqueness of difference: the cultural, ethnic, and religious heritages as well as the personal life journey of each individual. At the same time, it also honors the commonality that we share in our humanness, in our experiences of pain and sorrow, as well as moments of sheer delight and celebration. In the Christian community, it also recognizes the Christian story that unites us even though that story has been conveyed through different cultural lenses. The places of convergence and divergence are explored to better understand one another. Unity in the midst of diversity is sought with care and compassion. The challenge of difference is not denied or ignored but met head-on. The difficulty of cultural critique is never far from the surface. Difference, however, is also celebrated as being beneficial to the overall well-being of the community. The unexpected insights and glimpses into the holy that come in unforeseen ways because of difference are highly valued. God becomes less the property of a particular

group and more the source of this rainbow of difference that brings new revelations each day. The kin-dom vision of Pentecost is a constant image of the possibility of unity in diversity.

Living Multiculturally

What elements about ourselves, our attitudes, and our behaviors allow us to live faithfully in a multicultural context?[27]

Commitment to Cultural Diversity. One element is to recognize that from the very beginning of Christianity, cultural pluralism has been a part of the kin-dom vision and has been a reality among the members of the faith. The incarnation itself was a merger of the divine and human cultures.

Willingness to Suspend Judgment. Rather than immediately judging a particular action or belief, suspend automatic judgment for a moment. Reflect upon what offended you sufficiently to make that judgment. What of your own cultural assumptions or values was challenged or threatened by what the other person said or did? For example, Filipinos may show up late for church. You make an automatic judgment (based on your cultural orientation to time) that showing up fifteen minutes late for church is rude. In reality, however, these are cross-cultural misunderstandings. How can we suspend judgment until a deeper understanding is gained?

This is not to deny cultural critique of our own and other cultures, but to ensure the cultural critique is done from our best understanding of God's value system rather than critiquing from our own cultural value system. Withholding judgment from the Nazis would have perpetuated the Holocaust. Christians around the world had to use their biblical standards of love and justice and peace along with the commandment not to kill to judge Hitler's actions toward the Jews. Christians had to intervene and stop the "ethnic cleansing" carried out in the name of God. These are not always easy decisions, however. Look at the situations in Bosnia and Kosovo.

Yet it is difficult to separate our cultural values from our religious values, because our religious values are highly conditioned by our cultural values. In a multicultural community it is important to try to come to some decisions about common, core Christian values all can

---

[27]Law, *The Bush Was Blazing but Not Consumed,* 62–73, identifies five elements of what he calls "ethnorelative" responses to difference: (1) willingness to live in the uncertainty of being nonjudgmental; (2) learning to be "interpathic" to others who are different; (3) commitment to cultural pluralism; (4) learning to do contextual evaluation; and (5) living the spirituality of creative marginality.

agree to that will provide the standard by which human cultures will be critiqued.

It is inevitable, however, that miscommunication will happen in our daily interactions with persons of other cultures. When this happens, it is important for us to try not to immediately judge the other person, because our judgments come from our own culturally determined values. What is communicated by a person in one culture (calling someone by his or her first name) may be done out of friendship but be received as an insult, depending on one's cultural background. Suspending judgment on the values, beliefs, and practices of others gives us time to analyze our own responses (wanting to judge a person negatively) until we can learn more about the cultural values of the other.

Part of this willingness to suspend judgment is also a recognition that God is the ultimate judge of the values, beliefs, and practices of each culture. Living in the uncertainty of being nonjudgmental is being able to live with *ambiguity*. Charles Foster, in *We Are the Church Together,* speaks of multicultural congregations as those that "seek not to *resolve* but to *embrace* and *live faithfully* in ambiguity and change."[28] Living without preconditioned "absolutes," contemplating the possibility of a different worldview, and changing our attitudes and behavior are disconcerting and threatening. However, it can also be very exciting and promising.[29] Foster compares this "living with ambiguity" to Robert Bellah's *faith of loss:* "a relinquishing of some familiar, understandable, and previously treasured knowledge or meanings or assumptions, and a discovery that the world does not then fall apart but is somehow even more deeply meaningful than before."[30] Learning to live with ambiguity and being willing to suspend automatic judgment are crucial elements for living multiculturally.

Respecting in the Midst of Disagreement. Even when one disagrees with another, it is important to be able to step out of one's own cultural worldview and value system (as best one can) and try to understand another's perspective. It doesn't mean that we have to be converted to the belief or action of the other. It does mean, however, that we can respect and honor what is important to another even though, from our own cultural perspective, it is not meaningful or important.

---

[28]Charles R. Foster, *We Are the Church Together: Cultural Diversity in Congregational Life* (Valley Forge, Pa.: Trinity Press International, 1996), 156.

[29]Ibid., 160.

[30]Ibid., 167, referring to Robert N. Bellah, *Beyond Belief: Essays on Religion in a Post-Traditional World* (New York: Harper & Row, 1970), xix–xxi.

Learning to Celebrate Living on the Margins. Living on the margins can actually be a creative and enriching place to be. Many persons who come from a minority culture in this country live biculturally. They are "bridge" people who can move comfortably between two or more cultures. But persons of the majority culture can also live on the margins and be "bridge" people.

Jung Young Lee, in *Marginality: The Key to Multicultural Theology,* names Jesus as the ultimate marginal person.[31] Jesus was the bridge between God and humanity, between the Jews and the rest of the world, between the rich and the poor, between men and women. Jesus was comfortable at the tax collector's feast and communicating with persons with leprosy. He talked to the Samaritan woman at the well and listened to the request of the Roman centurion. Jesus embodies his call to us to live on the margins—"to be in the world but not of the world."

No matter who we are, no matter what culture we come from, in a multicultural context it is important for us all to learn how to be "bridge" people, how to live on the margins between cultures, comfortable in a variety of settings.

Summary

There are so many theories that come from politics and social psychology, ethnography and anthropology, ethics and theology, even theories about cultural diversity in businesses. Given the newness of these theories and the plethora of them, it is sometimes difficult to discern the wisdom available from them.

We are living in an in-between time when the old has passed away, but the new is still not fully defined, and this will never end. We will always be in this in-between time. Life is always in process. The tensions between what we all have in common and what makes us unique; the struggle between the notion of the equality of all cultures and the need for constant cultural critique; the controversy between stressing unity versus stressing diversity; and the tension between equal treatment of all versus preferential treatment of some as a way of rectifying past wrongs will all continue to be a part of the church and our society for years to come.

Multicultural congregations and communities are a reality, but we have not yet fully figured out how to live faithfully in this exciting

---

[31]Jung Young Lee, *Marginality: The Key to Multicultural Theology* (Minneapolis: Fortress Press, 1995), 99.

and challenging time. We are an "in-between" people in many ways. Ethicist Karen Lebacqz says that "mainline Protestant churches are living an in-between life—in between a remembered time of glory, when sanctuaries were filled to overflowing, and a possible demise."[32]

But we also live in between the "yet" and the "not yet" of Christian history. The kin-dom visions have come in the incarnation of Jesus Christ, and yet they have not yet been fully realized. Lebacqz continues: "In-between living is full of tension and ambiguity. I have come to think that the tensions and ambiguities of the in-betweenness are what we are meant to experience."[33]

Living in this "in-between" time will require much prayerful reflection, trial and error, faithful commitment to the task, and an ability to live with the tensions and ambiguities that are inevitable. Recognizing and embracing the other will bring us closer to kin-dom visions—the biblical visions that are unfettered by language of domination and hierarchy but rather are infused by our understanding that in the midst of our differences, we are all *kin* in the family of God.

In recognizing our kinship, however, we must also recognize the cultural values and customs that cause misunderstanding and miscommunication. It is to these "cultural complexities" that I now turn.

---

[32]Karen Lebacqz, *Word, Worship, World, & Wonder* (Nashville: Abingdon Press, 1997), 11.

[33]Ibid., 12.

CHAPTER THREE

Cultural Complexities

It is amazing how much culture influences our lives without many of us even being aware of it. Culture often determines not only what we eat and how we dress, but also what we think and how we act. Culture conditions everything from the way we make formal plans to the way we respond to various nonverbal behaviors. All cultures are rich and complex.

Confusion can happen when persons of different ethnic cultures participate in a common activity (e.g., worship). Often, few of the persons involved are fully aware of their own cultural values and influences, let alone the possibly conflicting cultural values and influences of persons from other culture(s).

In the worship services of multicultural congregations, denominational cultures and/or missionary cultures also influence the beliefs, behaviors, and expectations of persons in the congregation. Sometimes it is hard to sort out what is denominationally influenced, what is missionary influenced, what stems from one's ethnic cultural heritage, and what is simply personal preference.

Surface Culture and Primary Culture

There are some ethnic cultural elements, known as *surface culture*, that are easy to identify.[1] These include the foods people eat, the clothing people prefer to wear, and a culture's traditional music and

---

[1]Edward T. Hall, *Understanding Cultural Differences* (Yarmouth, Maine: Intercultural Press, 1990), 8.

dance. But how children identify animals by the sounds they make (European Americans say "cock-a-doodle-doo" for a rooster; Mexicans say "quiquiriqui" for a rooster) is also culturally determined. Another example is the way people count with their fingers. European Americans count 1, 2, 3 by placing one hand up in a fist handshape with palm facing outward and raising the first finger, then the middle finger, and then the "ring" finger. In Korea, however, the palm faces inward and all fingers are raised up to begin with. When counting, the thumb crosses over the palm for 1, then the first finger comes down over the thumb for 2, and finally the middle finger comes down over the thumb for 3. And in Nicaragua, one starts with a fist but with palm facing in, and to count, one raises the thumb first, then the first finger, and finally the middle finger to count 1, 2, 3. These last two illustrations may be inconsequential in the grand scheme of things, but it just goes to show that our basic assumptions about the sounds animals make or the way we teach children to count on their fingers are all influenced by one's culture.

There are other elements that seem confusing. For example, on the surface, one might notice that some parents do not keep a strict eye on their children. In worship, the children may be wandering up and down the aisles or climbing over the altar rail after church. What are not visible from an outsider's perspective, however, are the underlying cultural values in regard to child rearing that are operating.

In some cultures, children "misbehaving" during worship would be viewed as irresponsibility or lack of discipline on the part of the parents. These cultures believe that children are the responsibility of the parents and it is their job to watch out for and discipline their own children. In other cultures, however, not only are there different definitions about what constitutes "misbehaving" in church, but child rearing is seen as the responsibility of the whole community. It is every person's duty to participate in both affirming and disciplining the children of the community.[2]

There are even more complex cultural elements, however, that are so ingrained in persons from a particular culture that they are difficult to analyze. These elements are known as *primary culture*:[3] the rhythm of a particular culture, the breathing rate of different cultures (how many seconds there are between breaths), one's ability to read nonverbal behavior, one's orientation to time, and so on.

---

[2]Charles R. Foster, *We Are the Church Together: Cultural Diversity in Congregational Life* (Valley Forge, Pa.: Trinity Press International, 1996), 144.

[3]Hall, *Understanding Cultural Differences,* 8.

Throughout the rest of this chapter, these various ethnic cultural influences are applied to specific instances in the worship life of a multiethnic congregation. Following the discussion of *ethnic* cultural influences is a section dealing with *denominational* and *missionary* cultural influences that also pose challenges for the design and content of worship in multiethnic churches.

Ethnic Cultural Complexities
Worship Committees

A multiethnic congregation has made a strong attempt to recruit persons for the worship committee who represent the various cultures present in the congregation. The European American members speak up often and strongly. The members representing other cultures seldom speak up at all. The European American committee chair and the European American pastor want this to be a truly democratic process with equal representation by all, but it is difficult to get those from other cultures to articulate their opinions.

It may be the case that individual personalities on the committee may be shy or introverted, but there may be cultural factors operating as well. In many cultures, equality or equal representation are not values or expectations. Hierarchy and inequality are normal aspects of life in the countries of their birth. "People believe that there should be an order of inequality in the world."[4] In these cultures, most people know their "place" or their status in the ordering of things. The non-elite majority know they have virtually no power to make a difference. These cultures are known to have a ***high power distance,*** meaning there is a high or great distance between those with power and those without.

European Americans (along with Australians, Canadians, and Northern Europeans), however, operate in ***low power distance*** cultures that value equality and democracy. There is a lower or smaller distance between those with power and those without. We strive to eliminate inequalities in our country. Hierarchies exist but as a means to accomplish various tasks. More and more, the collegiality between superiors and subordinates is increased.[5]

---

[4]Eric H. F. Law, *The Wolf Shall Dwell with the Lamb* (St. Louis: Chalice Press, 1993), 19–22.
[5]Ibid.

In a worship committee meeting, the persons from other cultures may feel as if they have no power to make changes in the worship design or content. If they come from a country that believes and practices inequality and established hierarchical divisions, they may assume that the pastor (as head of the hierarchy) makes all the decisions, and the role of the laity is to follow and obey. They may be unclear about what behavior is expected of them as members of a committee that values equal representation and equal participation. Their silence may stem mainly from confusion and inexperience in that kind of setting.

Another cultural factor may be operating as well. European Americans are raised in a culture that highly values the individual. It is common for individuals not only to speak for themselves but to speak for others as well. But not all cultures are individualistically oriented like the United States. Many cultures are communally oriented.

Persons from communally-oriented cultures may not have the same sense of the "self," the individual "I," that European Americans do. They may find it difficult to understand what value a personal opinion would be to the worship committee. Speaking for the community would not be appropriate without talking with the community first. Being a representative *of* the community does not necessarily mean the person can speak *for* the community unless that person is an elder, chief, or other high-ranking person within that cultural group. Asking individual representatives from various cultures to serve on worship committees tends to operate more like tokenism. It is better to appoint several persons from the same culture to the committee so that there is a sense of communal identity.

Recruiting Participants

It is September and the European American pastor (with the help of the worship committee) has created a chart that lists all the Sundays between now and Epiphany (the first or second Sunday in January). Next to each Sunday are blank lines for people to sign up to read scripture, be a liturgist, provide donuts for coffee hour after church, be a greeter, and so on. The "old-timers" (mostly European American) sign up well in advance. It is difficult, however, to get some of the newer members from other cultures to sign up.

It may simply be that the persons are new and are not yet comfortable participating. However, it may also be a matter of **lead time.** "Different cultures expect different lead times for making appointments."[6] In the European American culture, we plan ahead. The future is a known quantity (excluding any natural disasters), and we work on the assumption that planning far ahead gives people more time to reserve those particular dates for participation in worship. European Americans consider it rude or imposing to ask someone at the last minute.

But for persons from the Middle East or from Japan, "two weeks is too far in advance–out of sight, out of mind–it is not important."[7] A Japanese pastor may see no problem with calling someone on Saturday to read scripture the next day, but if that layperson is European American, he or she may feel "put out" that the request was so last minute. Each culture varies in how much lead time is expected for making plans.

Liturgical Lay Leadership

A European American pastor asked a member of the congregation from Brazil to be the lay liturgist on the Sunday two weeks hence. The Brazilian member said yes. When that Sunday arrived, the person never showed up, and a substitute liturgist had to be recruited at the very last second as the processional began.

One of the most difficult cultural differences for European Americans to understand is *indirect speech,* or what is sometimes called *the relational yes.*[8] In some cultures, the relationship between two persons is so important that the person being asked would not openly refuse the request for fear of disappointing the other, hurting the other's feelings, or creating tension in the relationship. "Not to fulfill important persons' wishes is to cause them and yourself loss of face."[9] Even if the person knows that he or she will be out of town on that particular Sunday, the relationship at the time of the request (when the persons are in face-to-face communication) takes precedence over an unknown future date and time when the parties will not physically be present with one another.

In the European American culture, we prefer direct speech– "telling it like it is." We want people to be up front and honest with us. I've seen European American pastors so frustrated (and angry) about this "relational yes" that they just can't understand what lies

---

[6]Hall, *Understanding Cultural Differences,* 20.
[7]Ibid.
[8]Duane Elmer, *Cross-Cultural Conflict* (Downers Grove, Ill.: InterVarsity Press, 1995), 118.
[9]Ibid., 119.

behind it. To them, their well-laid plans are all for naught if people don't do what they say they are going to do. They begin to mistrust those from other cultures and eventually stop asking them to participate again. For those raised in the European American culture it can be very frustrating and difficult to understand, but even in the European American culture, there are times when we aren't completely honest, when we don't "tell it like it is." Instead we tell a "little white lie" in order to preserve a relationship. To protect the feelings of another and to maintain goodwill between us, one may *say* he has a meeting to go to when, in reality, he just doesn't feel like having dinner with the other person.

Persons within the same culture who regularly utilize this "relational yes" are accustomed to reading the indirect speech of the other. But cross-culturally, this skill is extremely difficult to develop. One multiethnic congregation in Southern California has built into its preparation process a "Plan B," or contingency plan, just in case those scheduled to sing a solo, read scripture, or be a liturgist fail to show.

Opening and Closing of Worship

A predominantly European American congregation has about 35 percent of its membership made up of persons recently arrived in America from various countries in Africa. Worship starts at 11:00 a.m., but the Africans show up fifteen to thirty minutes late. Some of the European Americans consider this rude and inappropriate, even lazy or unorganized, behavior on the part of the Africans.

In reality, however, the difficulty lies in different orientations to time. The European American culture is based on what is call *monochronic time.*[10] It is linear time. Our lives are dictated by moving from one occasion in time to another. We believe time is an entity that can be wasted, saved, spent, lost, made up, or killed. Think about the language we use in reference to time: "I *wasted* so much time." "I was just standing around *killing* time." "I *spent* way too much time at the doctor's office." "The computer *saves* so much time." It is a commodity that we preciously value, and it is considered rude and an imposition to intrude on another person's time.

But other cultures live in what is called *polychronic time.*[11] Polychronic time is more cyclical. Time is not a commodity, and it is not linear. You can't save it, waste it, or kill it. People are involved in

---

[10]Hall, *Understanding Cultural Differences,* 43–50.
[11]Ibid.

several things at one time. Relationships and involvement with people are much more important than keeping schedules and appointments. Schedules and appointments have to do with linear time. Those oriented to polychronic time don't think in terms of linear time in the same way that those oriented to monochronic time do.

In regard to worship, worship begins when the community has gathered, has greeted one another, and is "ready"–in synch with one another. And worship ends when the people are full of the Spirit and have exhausted all their praise and testimony and sharing of the word of God. It has nothing to do with a clock!

Music

A European American pastor and choir director have chosen a hymn with lyrics in both Spanish and English. They decide it is best for all to sing the first verse in English and then all sing the second verse in Spanish, and so on. The Hispanic members want to sing all the verses in Spanish, and if asked, many, if not most, European Americans would prefer to sing all the verses in English. But to have people singing in two languages simultaneously felt too discordant to the pastor and choir director.

One cultural value European Americans bring to music is **harmony.** In the above case study, harmony is about singing together in the same language so we all sound alike. When different people sing in different languages simultaneously, it sounds unharmonious—sometimes confusing and chaotic. In some cultures, however, singing in multiple languages is common. There may be two or three different languages common in the one culture. In a Haitian church, for instance, some people sing in French, others in Creole, and still others in English. This cacophony of sound seems unharmonious to those who hold European American values about harmony in music.

We value harmony in its many forms. We may be singing in unison, but that has its own "feel" of harmony to it. And if we are singing four-part harmony, it is a harmony that sounds right to European American ears. But each culture has a different understanding of musical harmony and what sounds right to the ear.

Rhythms are also different from culture to culture. Some tap their foot or clap on the downbeat, but others clap in threes to rhythms that have no up- or downbeat, which feels "uneven" or "off" to European American sensibilities.

Music can certainly be a controversial issue in many congregations, but there is also a richness that comes with learning the spiritual music that inspires the souls of various cultures around the globe.

Sharing of Joys and Concerns

It is common in this church for people to openly share both joys in their lives and prayer concerns. Births of babies, anniversary celebrations, recoveries from illness, new jobs, promotions, and graduations are all included in the "joy" section of this communal prayer time. Many people knew that a Japanese member of the congregation had recently received a journalism award at the newspaper he worked for. During the Sharing of Joys and Concerns, a woman behind him nudged him to share this with the entire congregation. When he didn't, she stood and shared it for him. The Japanese man felt not only embarrassed, but somewhat shamed.

The individualistic nature of the European American culture values opportunities to honor individuals for their endeavors and achievements. But in other cultures that are communally oriented, direct praise of an individual can cause great embarrassment, even shame. In a communal culture, it is openly recognized that no one exists without numbers of people who played an important role in that individual's success. The European American way of viewing success as the achievement of an individual alone is often viewed as inappropriate and ill-mannered.[12]

Prayer

During prayer time in a multiethnic mainline Protestant congregation, the African American organist played music to help foster a prayerful tone and attitude. Some older European American members of the congregation complained that it was distracting.

The reaction of the older European American members may be more than just "we (European American mainline Protestants) have never done it this way before." Orientations to *auditory space* vary from culture to culture. This is seen most clearly between generational cultures in this country today. Older European Americans tend to depend on auditory screening in order to concentrate. They require more auditory space—a cushion of quiet, so to speak. Unlike the teenagers of today who listen to music, watch TV, and do their homework at the same time, older generations were raised in a culture that screened out external auditory messages when a task required

---

[12]Elmer, *Cross-Cultural Conflict,* 48.

focus or concentration. The music that is being played in support of the prayer may make it more difficult for those requiring more auditory space to concentrate and internalize the words of the prayer. Auditory screening can also be found in ethnic cultures that are *low-context* cultures. In the European American "formal" culture, for example, it is common for bosses or professors to close their doors when meeting with someone. Having the door closed screens out the noises, conversations, and activities on the other side.

But there are *high-context* cultures where persons "thrive on being open to interruptions" in order to keep in touch with the various activities and developments surrounding them.[13] Auditory screening is seen as a detriment to keeping up-to-date on the relationships and connections that are so crucial to high-context communication. Minimal auditory space is needed to conduct any kind of business.

Passing the Peace

A European American female member of the congregation greeted a member from the Philippines during the Passing of the Peace. The Filipina returned the greeting with her eyes looking down and away from the woman. The European American left feeling that the Filipina was being unfriendly because her body language was closed and the Filipino woman would not make any eye contact.

The European American culture values open body language and direct *eye contact* as an important source of nonverbal communication. We "read" a person's body language and make certain assumptions, even judgments, based on our cultural definitions of the meaning of direct eye contact. If a person never looks us in the eye, we may make the assumption that the person is not invested in this relationship, is not really paying attention, or is trying to hide something.

In reality, however, many Asian cultures will not make direct eye contact as a sign of respect to the other. What was given by the Filipino woman as a gesture of respect was received as an insult because of different cultural values associated with eye contact.

Preaching

A European American pastor moves out of the pulpit to preach the sermon. Some Puerto Rican members of the congregation

---

[13]Hall, *Understanding Cultural Differences,* 12.

feel that preaching out of the pulpit is disrespectful to the word of God and the role of the preacher.

One conflicting expectation around preaching has to do with whether a pastor preaches in or out of the pulpit. It has become more and more popular in European American churches for the pastor to preach outside the pulpit—usually down front and closer to the congregation. It is an attempt to break down the assumed wall that divides the congregation and the preacher; an attempt to get closer to the congregation in a conversational style; an attempt to be more informal. Today in this culture *authority* is out, and *informality* is in. But there are persons from other cultures who highly value the authority of the preacher and the symbol of the pulpit as the place where a word from God can be heard.

In saying that, there is also a cultural assumption that the preacher speaks a word from God. In the European American culture today, many don't want that burden or responsibility. Preachers speak the truth as they know it and try to be as faithful as possible, but the old "herald" model of preaching has gone by the wayside in many European American pulpits (at least mainline Protestant pulpits). It is still very much alive in other cultures, however.

Announcements

The lay liturgist calls upon a committee chairperson by his first name to make an announcement. The chairperson is Chinese and is insulted by the informal use of his first name in the public gathering of worship. He feels disrespected.

In the European American culture, the informal *use of first names* is an attempt at collegiality and even intimacy. It is a way to signal that we want to get to know you better; we want to be your friend. But in other cultures, the use of the first name is a definite sign of *dis*respect. In some cultures it is related to status, age, and position. One would never call an older person of higher status by her or his first name. First names are reserved for family and a few close, intimate friends.

In the emerging African American culture during the slave period and years later, African Americans were only called by their first names or were called "boy" or "hey you." Their identities were stripped from them. They were not allowed to keep last names. Names that the masters couldn't pronounce were changed. Using last names today affirms their individual and familial identity and shows respect.

Different cultural assumptions around naming can create tremendous discomfort. The same act (the informal use of one's first name) can be given in love and friendship by one culture and received as disrespect in another culture.

Many newcomers from various cultures had requested additional opportunities (alternative times and meeting places) for Bible study classes. During the announcement time in worship (called "Educational and Missional Opportunities"), the European American associate pastor announced that three new Bible study classes would be starting that week. Each one was offered at a different time (one early morning before work at a downtown coffee shop, one in the evening at a parishioner's home, and one late afternoon at the church). Despite the diversity of people who requested more Bible study times, few persons (other than European Americans) showed up the first week.

The way various cultures **communicate important announcements** is another issue that arises at this time in the worship service. European Americans tend to print announcements in the bulletin or newsletter and announce important events during worship. This is usually sufficient to inform people that their presence is appreciated and valued. However, in other cultures, if a person's presence is wanted and valued at a particular event, the invitation will be personal—through face-to-face communication or at least a personal phone call. Communicating information and extending invitations to people to participate in various activities can also vary from culture to culture.[14]

People Greeting Each Other after Worship

After worship, a European American male greets a Middle Eastern male member of the congregation who was sitting behind him. They move into the aisle to continue their conversation. The Middle Eastern man stands within a foot of the European American man, who begins to feel very uncomfortable. The European American man backs away, but the Middle Eastern man just moves closer.

Each culture has boundaries on what is considered *safe personal space.* For European Americans it is about two to three feet. For some

[14]Charles R. Foster, *Embracing Diversity: Leadership in Multicultural Congregations* (Washington, D.C.: Alban Institute, 1997), 34.

cultures, however, it can be one foot to five feet. If we are greeting a person in church and the person stands five feet from us, European Americans tend to label them as aloof or not interested in getting to know us. If a person greets us with a hug and continues to stay one foot from our face, the automatic European American response is that the person is too pushy. Or we may become defensive or even fearful about our personal safety and make a note to avoid that person in the future. In reality, however, these are just different cultural orientations to safe and appropriate personal space.

Pastor Greeting the People after Worship

The European American male pastor greets many people with a hug as they process out of the sanctuary after worship. A Filipino man (a well-known and active layperson) resists the pastor's hug and withdraws. The pastor feels as if he may have caused some unintentional offense.

Learning how to greet persons from other cultures is an education in and of itself. What is appropriate? a handshake, a hug, a bow, a kiss on the cheek, or a kiss on each cheek like the French or the Swiss or the Russians? Is the greeting only appropriate between two men, or two women, or between a man and a woman? Does the greeting gesture mean the same thing when used with persons of the same age, different ages, equal status, or unequal status? There are many factors to consider.

In some cultures it is appropriate for the same sex to hug in public but not for members of the opposite sex. In other cultures it is the opposite. It is acceptable for the opposite sex to hug or exchange kisses in public but not members of the same sex.

A bow may be appropriate in the Korean, Japanese, or Chinese cultures, but since the pastor is viewed as having a higher status than the laity, it may not be appropriate for the pastor to bow to the laity—or at least not to bow too low. Cambodians often greet each other by placing their hands together in a "praying hands" form and raising their hands so that the thumbs are touching the nose/forehead area and then giving a slight nod of the head. Filipino youth may greet the pastor by touching the back of the pastor's hand to their forehead. This is called "mano pa" and is considered a greeting of respect.

The best way for the pastor and the congregation to figure out this complex area of greeting one another is to ask each person what is appropriate and preferred.

Denominational and Missionary Complexities
Opening Words of Worship

A responsive call to worship is led by the liturgist to open the worship service. Some in the congregation are a little unsettled, feeling as if worship has not officially begun yet.

Many cultures influenced by nineteenth-century European and American missionaries are confused by calls to worship that use contemporary secular language in a responsive form. For them, the only appropriate way to open worship is by words from scripture—usually from the Psalms in a proclamation form.

Apostles' Creed

The Apostles' Creed was included in the worship service of a multiethnic Protestant church that was historically European American. Some of the newer members from Latin America asked why this church was using a "Catholic ritual in a Protestant church."[15]

In some cultures, Protestants associate the Apostles' Creed and printed prayers with the dominant (and in their opinion, oppressive) Roman Catholic Church of their native country. One way of distinguishing the Protestants from the Roman Catholics in these countries is the elimination of any printed liturgy in Protestant worship. For many people, in order for the service to be spirit filled and spirit led, the prayers and liturgy must emerge spontaneously, or at least extemporaneously, from the pastor or worship leader. Extemporaneous liturgies and prayers, then, become the norm for many Protestants who come from Catholic-dominated countries.

Prayer

The previous European American pastor of a multiethnic United Methodist congregation in Falls Church, Virginia, tells this story:

At six o'clock one Good Friday morning, he received a phone call from a European American teacher of their English as a Second Language class. She was calling from the church office where she was photocopying material for her class. She wanted the pastor to know that she had called the police because she heard "wailing and thumping" coming from the sanctuary. It sounded to her as if someone was out of control, banging

---

[15]Stephen A. Rhodes, *Where the Nations Meet: The Church in a Multicultural World* (Downers Grove, Ill.: InterVarsity Press, 1998), 176.

things, and possibly destroying the sanctuary. She assumed it was a homeless person. The pastor asked if she had actually gone in to see if this was indeed the case. She said no because she was somewhat fearful. After some thought, the pastor said that there may be another explanation. Some Korean men come to the church early in the morning to pray. She quickly hung up, checked it out, and canceled the police![16]

The Korean men were indeed praying in the sanctuary, but the prayer form that was meaningful to them that morning was a form known as "Tong Song Kido"–roughly translated, it means "praying aloud." During Tong Song Kido, persons pray their individual prayers aloud simultaneously. In addition, whether sitting or kneeling, they often rock their bodies back and forth in a rhythmic motion. If the Koreans were sitting in a chair, the chair itself might rock, thereby thumping the wooden floor. The overall effect is a cacophony of voices that ebb and flow in both volume and rhythm. When the individual's prayer is confessional or mournful (as on Good Friday), it may sound like wailing to an unaccustomed ear. Someone raised in a denominational culture where prayer was silent or at least offered in a quiet voice never would have recognized the sounds of Tong Song Kido as prayer.

A variation of this form of prayer can be found in the European American culture in congregations with Pentecostal roots. Individual prayers are said aloud simultaneously but without the rise and fall in volume and rhythm.

While Tong Song Kido is a comfortable and very meaningful prayer form for many Koreans and others who come from a Pentecostal background, mainline Protestant European Americans participating in this style of prayer often feel self-conscious and awkward. Part of it has to do with our value of privacy; it is uncomfortable to voice our private thoughts to God aloud for all to hear. Mainline Protestant European Americans' reactions to this type of prayer form may also reflect our value of harmony. The cacophony of voices feels unharmonious and even chaotic to our sensibilities.

In multicultural congregations, it is important to learn about the various prayer forms that are meaningful to the congregants so that the misunderstanding that happened in the example above can be averted.

It is the custom of this historically European American congregation to sit during the Prayer of Confession. It does not

---

[16]Ibid., 158–59.

seem to be a problem for the European American and African American members of the congregation. However, the Vietnamese American members prefer to stand.

Most Southeast Asian Protestant Christians are highly influenced by the Christian Missionary Alliance denomination. They were and are the strongest missionaries in Vietnam, Cambodia, and Laos. To persons from these countries, the theology and worship practices of the Christian Missionary Alliance denomination are what is *Christian* to them. It is not a matter of one Christian denomination's approach to Christianity versus another's. It is the difference between Christianity and Buddhism.

In the Christian Missionary Alliance church, the people stand for all prayers. The people collectively respond in Vietnamese at the end of any prayer with the words "In the name of Jesus Christ, Amen." They may find it disrespectful to sit for any prayer time.

Music

A Filipino member of the congregation is scheduled to sing a solo on Sunday. The Filipino wants to use taped music in the background during the solo. The European American musician/choir director insists on using live music—playing the organ to accompany the soloist. The Filipino soloist shows up on Sunday with a cassette tape to play over the church's sound system.

Traditionally, European American churches valued live music accompanied by organ or piano and this value was taken by missionaries all over the world. But there are cultures that don't have organs or pianos or can't get organs or pianos out to the islands on which they live. Each culture has dealt with this differently. Christians in the Tongan islands chose not to use any instruments. Filipinos in the latter part of this century often use taped music in the background to accompany the choir or soloist. It is not only common and acceptable in the Filipino Christian community, it is often preferable.

Preaching

After worship, many persons were complimenting the preacher on such a fine sermon (which lasted about seventeen minutes). A Mexican American member of the congregation shook hands with the pastor and said, "What happened? You were just getting started."

Today's American culture has been greatly influenced by a multimedia, TV-oriented society. People's attention spans have dwindled to the ten minutes of programming on TV between the commercial breaks. Sermons have become shorter and shorter in this country. But in other cultures, it is common for a sermon to last forty-five minutes to more than an hour. A fifteen-minute sermon seems like an introduction. Most European American congregations, however, would not sit through a forty-five minute sermon, let alone one lasting more than an hour. After twenty minutes, they would be checking their watches because of their monochronic orientation to time.

A European American pastor preached from a full manuscript one Sunday. A few members from other cultures made comments after church: "I guess it was a really busy week for you." "Didn't have much time to prepare this week, huh?"

Another conflicting issue in preaching is whether the preacher uses notes or a manuscript, or preaches extemporaneously. In most Roman Catholic and mainline Protestant European American churches, using extensive notes or a manuscript is a sign that the pastor has done the homework and is prepared for the sermon. They certainly want an animated delivery and not someone reading a paper, but still, the presence of notes implies that the preacher is prepared.

In other cultures (e.g., ethnic, denominational, and missionary cultures), however, using notes or a manuscript is not only a sign of being *un*prepared, it is also a sign of being unwilling to be led by the Holy Spirit.

Sermon Talk-Back Sessions

A recent immigrant from Africa talked with one of the European American pastors about having a time when people could discuss the texts and/or topic of the sermon. The pastors took this recommendation seriously and started a sermon talk-back time after church on Sundays. Neither the man who made the suggestion nor any other African members showed up for these conversations.

European Americans have little problem conversing about—often critiquing—the pastor or the sermon. For persons from other cultures, however, it is inappropriate to discuss or critique what they consider to be a "sacred speech act" once it has been delivered.

It may be better to have a Bible study earlier in the week that discusses the texts for the upcoming sermon. In that way, a discussion can take place on the texts and/or topic for the sermon, but it can be applied *to* the sermon rather than a talk-back or critique *after* the sacred speech act has occurred.

Pouring the Libation

A traditional African American congregation has many members who have recently emigrated from Africa. The African American congregation has made attempts in recent years to be more "Afro-centric" in its worship. On All Saints Day, the ritual of Pouring the Libation was used. As water was poured from a gourd into a plant on the altar, people named their ancestors who had died. Some of the newer African members of the congregation were upset that the Pouring the Libation ritual was used in Christian worship.

Pouring the Libation has become more and more common in African American congregations. It may be used on All Saints Day, or during African American History Month to name African American leaders throughout history, or during weddings to name the ancestors of the bride and groom. It is a way that African Americans have tried to reclaim their African roots.

However, many missionaries in Africa condemned this ritual as "ancestor worship" and forbade its use in Christian churches in Africa. Recent African immigrants, influenced by the missionary culture, may find the use of this ritual in Christian worship to be offensive.

Expressive Versus Quiet Behavior in Worship

A Haitian family from a Methodist church in Haiti joined a United Methodist African American church in their new neighborhood. During the singing, the people sitting around them tapped their feet and moved back and forth to the music. Shortly after the sermon began, the African Americans actively participated in the "call and response" form of preaching. Words of encouragement such as "well" or words of affirmation such as "amen" or "preach it" provided an underlying support for the preacher. The Haitian family was uncomfortable with such overt expressive behavior in worship. The color of their skin blended well in this congregation, but the style of worship was not their liturgical home.

The difference between overtly expressive styles of worship and more sedate, quiet styles of worship may be the biggest challenge multiethnic congregations face. In some ethnic and denominational cultures, worship is not worship without involving the entire body in praise to God. Moving, dancing, clapping, and tapping the feet are a natural part of worship. In a Ghanaian church in Brooklyn, New York, members dance up the aisle to the front of the church to put their monetary contributions in the offering bowl or tithing box. Dance is integral to their praise of God.

In other ethnic and denominational cultures, however, the tone of worship is much more sedate. The body is involved and the mind is focused on the worship and praise of God, but there is very little overt verbal or bodily participation unless it is scripted (e.g., reading a prayer, singing a hymn, closing one's eyes, etc.).

The divisions between the two styles of worship, however, are not necessarily ethnically or racially determined. Denominational background plays a much stronger influence. There are white European American Pentecostals who are extremely expressive in worship and African American Anglicans or Haitian United Methodists who are extremely sedate during their participation in worship.

Summary

While this chapter has focused on ethnic, denominational, and cultural misunderstandings, similar communication confusions can arise between other subcultures within our society: generational cultures, class cultures, gay and lesbian culture, deaf culture, and so on.

Culture truly does influence the way we think and act. But humans are also very adaptable, and many learn to move in and out of two or more cultures with ease. For economic survival alone, many persons from other cultures assimilate to Western orientations to time, the use of direct speech, and more direct eye contact–at least in the business world. But in the spiritual world of the multicultural church, one will find persons all along the spectrum of cultural accommodation. Some will cling to their native cultural values and practices (especially if there are others in the congregation from the same culture). Others want to be "Americanized" as quickly as possible and try to do things "the American way." And still others are anywhere in between on this spectrum of cultural accommodation.

These various cultural complexities definitely pose challenges to multicultural congregations, but they should not overwhelm the pastors or congregations to the point that they lose sight of the kin-dom vision that draws these diverse groups of Christians together in the first place.

In many multicultural congregations, any individual ethnic or denominational culture's particular preferences cannot be judged as more worthy, more holy, or a faster avenue to encountering God than another. People must be open to allowing the various members to participate in the manner most meaningful for them without automatic judgment one way or another. The challenge is getting the different expectations and preferences out in the open. Once they are out in the open, the pastors and lay leaders can work on ways of negotiating a balance in the design, content, and style of worship. Hopefully this emerging worship will, over time, lead to the creation of culturally-conscious worship that this unique, multiethnic (and often multidenominational in backround) community of faith can affirm and celebrate.

CHAPTER FOUR

Shared Stories, Shared Story

Given the extremely diverse cultural complexities raised in chapter 3, but keeping always before us the unifying kin-dom vision of Pentecost, how does a multicultural congregation approach the central act of worship? Why do diverse people gather to worship? What does Christian worship[1] symbolize for the various cultures around the world?

Worship's Story

Throughout the centuries and around the world, people have tried to articulate what worship is and what worship does:

- Worship is giving honor and praise to God.
- Worship effects a new relationship between God and each individual present.[2]
- Worship mediates God's grace to us.
- Worship expresses and embodies God's reality and presence.

---

[1] I am using the term *worship* in the traditional sense. It refers to an entire worship service that involves participation of the people of God. Today in some contemporary worship settings, the service is divided into "worship" and "teaching." In these contexts, the term *worship* is limited to the extended time of singing at the beginning of the service.

[2] Andy Langford, *Transitions in Worship: Moving from Traditional to Contemporary* (Nashville: Abingdon Press, 1999), 62.

- Worship "offers Christ for human acceptance."[3]
- Worship is the communal living out of the kin-dom on earth.
- Worship empowers us to move out into the world as disciples of God's love.
- Worship is the "offering of our whole selves to God."[4]
- Worship is the event in the present where God's past acts of salvation history and the living out of God's future eschatological promises come together.

While each congregation (influenced by its culture, denominational and local history, and current theology) may emphasize one of these understandings of worship more than others, in reality, the depth of the worship experience has the potential of holding these diverse meanings in tension and in unity.

These various understandings of worship point to both a vertical relationship[5] with God and a horizontal relationship with one another. In the vertical relationship, we give honor and praise to God, we offer our whole selves to God and develop a new relationship with God, and God blesses us with grace and strength and assurance. In the horizontal relationship with one another, we work together toward the communal living out of God's kin-dom on earth, empowering one another to be disciples of God's love. Notice that both the horizontal relationship and the vertical relationship work both ways. It is we who honor God and God who inspires us. Horizontally, I am a disciple empowered to bring God's love to others ("the Peace of God be with you"), but I am also graced by God as I receive the love and friendship of another ("and also with you"). We offer our whole selves to God, God offers Godself to us, and we offer ourselves and our experience of God to others in love throughout the continuous drama of worship and life. Offering one's whole self to God, however, implies bringing one's culture and one's culturally-influenced ways of relating to both God and one another into worship.

The horizontal aspect of worship is also present in the *design* of worship. "Worship" as the subject of each sentence listed above is not some abstract concept, but rather is humanly designed and

---

[3]Ibid., 67.

[4]Marjorie Hewitt Suchocki, *The Whispered Word: A Theology of Preaching* (St. Louis: Chalice Press, 1999).

[5]By the use of the term *vertical,* I do not mean to imply that God is only "above" us, only transcendent. I am a strong believer in the immanence of God. I understand God to be everywhere at all times. But for lack of more articulate vocabulary to describe these two relational aspects of worship, I will use *vertical* to describe the offering of ourselves and our praises to God and God's offering of grace and blessing to us.

created–hopefully prayerfully designed and spiritually guided in its creation, but nevertheless, designed by faithful beings. It is designed by humans for other humans in (what should be) our best attempts to create an environment, a liturgical event, that will facilitate the various purposes of worship: a sacred space to collectively honor God, a time to be renewed in our relationship with God, to experience a communal living out of God's kin-dom on earth, to be empowered to be disciples of justice in the world.

The words to the liturgy itself may have been created by faithful Christians many centuries ago, passed down from generation to generation, still repeated in denominations that globally share a common "prayer book." Or some of these ancient texts may be borrowed, along with contemporary texts, even texts written for a particular Sunday to be included in a bulletin for corporate prayer. Or the liturgy may be created extemporaneously during the worship service itself.

Even in those denominations that follow a "prayer book" for the liturgy, the pastor still decides what to preach, and the pastor or music director or worship team still chooses what hymns or songs to sing as well as any other artistic offerings (choir anthems, solos, liturgical dance, string quartet, mariachi guitars and maracas, African drums, etc.). And in those congregations that come from a more "free church" tradition, the order as well as the content of the service can vary from week to week. The intentional care taken in the design and content of the liturgy is crucial to facilitating both the vertical and horizontal relationships intricately woven into Christian worship.

It is easy to understand how the horizontal aspects of worship (ministry to, with, and for one another in the church and in various communities beyond the church) in a multicultural context might need more attention, since the people come from such diverse cultures, backgrounds, and faith journeys. The fostering of these relationships is necessary for true community to develop.

However, the vertical relationship of worship must also be given serious attention in multicultural congregations. All of us have certain preferred ways (often culturally and/or denominationally determined ways) of honoring and praising God, as well as certain songs, prayers, and postures of worship that facilitate our experiencing of God's presence, our reception of God's many graces.

In multicultural contexts, the culturally-influenced ways of honoring God and receiving inspiration from God may be extremely diverse. One cannot assume the people have a common "shared story" or common understanding of the structure, content, or style of worship.

In Roman Catholic, Orthodox, and Anglican/Episcopalian churches, the common *liturgy* provides a shared story. Wherever one goes in the world, the liturgy is basically the same; it is recognizable as the common bond across extremely diverse cultures. The structure and content of the liturgy is the shared memory within the community.

In other congregations, it is not the liturgical content and structure that all share in common, but a larger story that binds the people together. In a predominantly gay/lesbian/bisexual community, it is the history and contemporary issues of that subculture that join the people together. They have a shared story as gay/lesbian/bisexual people. In the deaf church, the experience of deafness unites them across ethnic cultures. There are some multicultural congregations whose primary ministry is toward the homeless population. It is the homeless subculture that transcends the racial or ethnic boundaries. Military culture provides a broader shared story for multicultural congregations on military bases.

However, in many local Protestant multicultural congregations, the people share neither a common liturgy nor a common subculture. The lack of a shared story, a common culture, can be a stumbling block as the people join in worship together. Certainly racism, ethnocentrism, cross-cultural miscommunication, and unequal power dynamics contribute to the complex nature of multicultural congregations, but the lack of shared experiences, shared expectations, and a shared memory poses a unique challenge for the worship life of these congregations. Having a shared story, creating one, or finding out what is shared in common among the various constituencies in a multicultural congregation is crucial for the welfare and growth of the faith community.

Creating a Shared Story at Pentecost

In the kin-dom vision of Pentecost, people from different countries and cultures who were speaking different languages were touched by the Holy Spirit in a way that gave them the ability and sensitivity to listen to one another and also to learn from one another. Most of these people were Jews who had come to Jerusalem for **Shavuoth**–the Feast of Weeks–to offer the new grain of the harvest to God. Despite their national diversity, however, they shared a common Jewish identity as the people of God, the heirs of the promise. They had a shared story.

But then Gentiles became converted who didn't share the same Jewish God or Hebrew story of salvation history. They were novices to the Hebrew faith and new converts along with many other Jews to the story of Jesus. They didn't share any collective story or memory.

And yet, these many individuals with different cultural, political, and religious histories created a community in the midst of their diversity. The central story of Jesus' life, death, and resurrection became part of the collective memory of this new group. In living in close community, worshiping together, studying together, eating together, and caring for one another's needs, they created new memories that all had in common; they created a new, shared story.

Different Interpretations of the Story

Like the people after Pentecost, creating a shared story with a multicultural congregation is essential. It's harder in today's world, because, unlike the afterglow of Pentecost, persons in multicultural congregations don't worship together daily. They don't live together or eat all their meals with one another, and they don't share their possessions with one another. It is still possible, however, to create a true community in the midst of great diversity. It just means that creating a new shared story, a collective memory, takes more time and conscious initiative to develop.

Christian worship presupposes a shared story: a story about God's acts in salvation history; a story about the life, ministry, death, and resurrection of Jesus; a story about God's future–the kin-dom vision. Each culture shares the same plot of this Christian story, but it has been and still is mediated through a particular language system, a particular culture, a particular worldview, and a particular value system. So when Christians from various cultural, linguistic, and denominational backgrounds worship together, the interpretations of the same shared story can be diverse.

In some situations, textual interpretations can be contradictory, as in the interpretation of the slave texts in the Bible by the white slave owners and the African slaves, or the interpretation of texts by white South Africans and black South Africans during apartheid. In other situations they can be rich and exciting new insights into the texts.

The biblical texts that talk about "shame" are barely noticed in the Western world. But in shame-based cultures, these texts take on a whole different significance because of the cultural lenses through which these texts are interpreted (Gen. 2:25; 3:7; Rom. 9:33; 10:11; 2 Cor. 7:14; 9:4; Heb. 2:11; 11:16; 12:2; 1 Pet. 2:6).[6] When a lawyer asks Jesus, "And who is my neighbor?" Jesus doesn't give a direct answer (Lk. 10:29). Instead, Jesus tells a story. Jesus' use of parables

---

[6]Duane Elmer, *Cross-Cultural Conflicts* (Downers Grove, Ill.: InterVarsity Press, 1995), 139.

and sayings is interpreted by some cultures as an affirmation of their culture's way of resolving conflict through indirect speech forms rather than direct confrontation that could bring shame on another. Direct confrontation between the parties involved is the preferred method of problem solving in the European American culture. But there are many cultures that use *mediators* to resolve conflicts so relationships are not broken. Mediators are also used to facilitate relational contracts (marriages) and business contracts. When the biblical texts that talk about Moses as a mediator (Gal. 3:19–20; Ex. 32:30–32; Num. 12:6–8), the prophets as mediators (Deut. 18:18–23), the priests of the Hebrew people as mediators (Ex. 28:1; Lev. 9:7; 16:6; Heb. 5:1–4), and especially Jesus as mediator (Jn. 3:17; Heb. 7–8; 1 Tim. 2:5–6) are viewed through the lenses of a culture where mediators are necessary for the goodwill of the community, these texts take on new meaning.[7] Textual interpretation varies depending on one's cultural orientations.

Individualistic cultures like the United States tend to interpret texts that are communally oriented as individually directed: "For God so loved the world..." is often interpreted "For God so loved me" or "For God so loved you" when working to convert another.[8] But many in communally-oriented cultures interpret these texts from a collective mind-set: God doesn't pick favorites; there is no hierarchy with God, no chosen elite; all are one in Christ Jesus.

The biblical story has also been interpreted through different languages. It is difficult enough to determine the meaning(s) of the Hebrew and Greek texts working in the original languages. And despite the depth of biblical scholarship, there are still some texts that are ambiguous. When those texts are translated into modern languages, there are many choices that have to be made and much *interpretation* (rather than straight translation, or transliteration) that takes place.

When these texts are interpreted in the life of a multicultural congregation, other problems can arise. One pastor asked the congregation to turn to one another and say, "God loves you and I love you." Like the Greek language, the Spanish language has different words for "love" depending on the relationship. In English, "love" is used in relationship to ice cream, jazz, basketball, one's child, spouse, and God. In many Latin American cultures, it is awkward and inappropriate for someone to say, "I love you" to a stranger or even an acquaintance.

---

[7]Ibid., 77–79.
[8]Ibid., 138.

The Spanish language also translates the first words of the prologue to the gospel of John as "*En el principio era el Verbo*" ("In the beginning was the Word").[9] Notice the translator translated the Greek word *logos* to mean "Verb" rather than the English translation of "Word," which in Spanish would have been *la Palabra*. The Spanish translator interpreted *logos* as an active word–a verb. This gives a very action-oriented connotation to Jesus as the *Word*.

There are some cultures that didn't have the word *resurrection* in their native language. When the Christians arrived, they had to borrow combinations of words from the native language to identify the closest meaning of *resurrection* (e.g., transliteration from Korean is "live again.") In American Sign Language, the sign for Christ is the same as "king" except the hand forms a "C" instead of a "K." How the texts are interpreted into the various languages implies a particular theological interpretation that has taken place in the translation (e.g., Jesus as a "Word" who lives in action the words of God, or Christ is like a king). The same biblical story is interpreted through cultural lenses.

One's faith journey is also lived out in particular cultural contexts. Living one's faith as a first-generation Christian in Taiwan surrounded by a Buddhist family and Buddhist society is very different from someone who was born to Christian parents, grandparents, and great-grandparents in a country whose coins are stamped by the government "In God we Trust." Those who have lived through persecution as Christians in Muslim-dominated countries have a collective story of faith that is very different from the faith journeys of many Americans.

So while worship is rooted in a collective shared story (the biblical story and the story of shared faith journeys), since these stories are culturally influenced, they may not be held in common by members of a multiethnic congregation.

What does hold the congregation together in its initial stages? What common cord binds such diverse people together? The kindom vision of Pentecost gives each of us the confidence to believe that we are all children of God; that we belong to the body of Christ, the family of God. In extremely diverse multiethnic congregations, the primary bond that is shared by all is the understanding that we all come before God in worship as members of the family of God.

We also share basic elements of the liturgy in common. While the various elements of liturgy may take on a different form (responsive call to worship rather than proclamation of a Psalm text, differing prayer forms, music styles, etc.), most cultures share basic worship

---

[9] *La Santa Biblia,* Reina-Velera (Mexico City: Sociedad Biblica International, 1977), 801.

elements in common: a gathering of the people, some sort of opening of worship, prayer, praise (often through music, but in the deaf culture it can be other art forms), reading of a text(s), proclamation (or "teaching" in some worship contexts), baptism of people into the community of faith, celebration of holy communion (eucharist), and some form of bringing the worship service to a close.

Since worship is the activity that most people in a multicultural congregation share in common on a weekly basis, worship becomes a crucial (but certainly not the only) place for this diverse group of people to develop a common memory, a shared story. While there are elements of worship that we hold in common and while we are all children of God and members of the body of Christ, people in a multicultural congregation may not share a common understanding of "appropriate" ways to honor and praise God. They may not share a common experience of what songs, prayer forms, and worship postures bring inspiration from God. Therefore, it is important in diverse contexts to foster a shared story, a common memory.

Creating a Shared Story, a Common Memory

While experts in the area of congregational studies assert that every congregation has its own "culture,"[10] this concept takes on a slightly different meaning in multiethnic congregations that take seriously the cultures represented by the various members. By all sharing their cultures, their histories and faith journeys, as well as the ways they traditionally praise God and the ways that God inspires them through certain songs and prayer forms, a "third" culture emerges out of shared memories that blends elements from each of the cultures present.

In the Mexican and Mexican American culture, they deeply understand the concept of "mestizaje"–it is the blending of the native Mexicans and the Spanish who conquered Mexico. These "mestizo" people have preserved aspects of their individual cultural pasts but have also internalized aspects of the culture of the other. A third culture has been created–a mestizo culture. Mexican Americans use this concept to deal with being persons of Mexican heritage living within the American culture. A new blending is taking place, and a "third" or maybe "fourth" culture is being created in the Mexican American community.

---

[10]Nancy T. Ammerman, Jackson W. Carroll, Carl S. Dudley, and William McKinney, *Studying Congregations: A New Handbook* (Nashville: Abingdon Press, 1998), 78–104.

Culturally-conscious worship works in a similar way. It helps preserve aspects of individual cultural pasts but also provides opportunities to experience and internalize aspects of another culture. Culturally-conscious worship facilitates the emergence of this "third" culture by fostering ways in which the various individual stories are shared by all to become a new common story.

Biblical Images

Many leaders in multicultural congregations work at creating a shared story by drawing from biblical texts, themes, and images that become an organizing core for the church's ministry. The diverse ways that persons from various cultures have interpreted a particular text may be offered in a sermon, but more likely, the text is interpreted through a *multicultural* lens (rather than any particular cultural lens), so it becomes a shared interpretation for that multicultural community. Various texts provide images and metaphors that multicultural congregations use as core symbols that organize the life of the congregation.

First Corinthians 12:12–26 depicts the body of Christ, an image so strong that we cannot say to any member of the body, "We have no need of you." From Galatians 3:28, a congregation affirms that regardless of nationality, religious background, or gender, "We are all one in Christ Jesus." Revelation 7:9–11 provides us with another kin-dom vision, a vision of a multitude so great that no one could count; a vision of people from every nation, from all tribes and peoples and languages, standing before the Lamb of God. In Ephesians 2:14 we realize that Jesus has already broken down the dividing wall, the hostility that exists between two specific groups with differing backgrounds and histories. And Luke 14:16–24 reminds us that all persons, regardless of their race or class or physical ability, are welcome at God's banquet table.

Whatever text(s) the congregation chooses as the cornerstone or building blocks of its multicultural ministry, the regular reference to these texts helps create a shared story, a shared memory for multicultural congregations to continue the work of building their life together. Eventually, a new congregational culture is created out of the diversity of persons present who are united by common identities as children of God, heirs of God's promise, members of the family of God, the community of the faithful. The pastor certainly isn't going to preach on these texts every Sunday, and yet these themes and images often find their way into one aspect of worship or another.

Visual Art

Visual art can also nurture a sense of shared story. At Culmore United Methodist Church in Falls Church, Virginia, "forty percent [of the congregation] are Anglo, thirty percent are Filipino; fifteen percent are African; ten percent are Latin American; and five percent are other nationalities, including Jamaican, Cambodian, Korean, Indonesian, and Asian Indian."[11] Prominently displayed in the sanctuary is a large banner that displays an image of a church building and a globe showing the various continents of our world. Cords of thread emanate from the center of the church outward to the various parts of the world represented by the members in the congregation. Visually this affirms a shared story: The tremendously diverse journeys of each person present has led them from all over the globe to gather together in this one place to worship God and to be a faithful community in response to the needs of the world.

Music

Music is another liturgical element used by multicultural congregations to establish a common bond. Singing together unifies the various spirits into a common offering. But singing together only works to create a sense of unity if as many people as possible can participate. In multicultural congregations, there is the possibility that the people won't share a common hymnody. Churches have taken different paths in their use of music to create a common bond, a shared story. I want to examine four different models of the ways congregations use music to create a shared memory. While I am well aware that worship (particularly in multicultural congregations) is always in process and that many multicultural worship services tend to be some sort of blend of these various models, I want to depict them in their extreme possibilities in order to analyze what effect each has on the vertical and horizontal relationships of worship and what theology can be (intentionally or unintentionally) proclaimed.

(1) The most common model is basically an assimilation model. The majority culture is welcoming of persons from other cultures, but those persons are expected to assimilate into the already existing worship. The music that is important for members of the majority culture is music that expresses their praises to God and also brings them inspiration from God in that vertical relationship of worship. While it may ignore or even deny the traditional vertical avenues meaningful to persons of other cultures (what is appropriate praise

---

[11]Stephen A. Rhodes, *Where the Nations Meet: The Church in a Multicultural World* (Downers Grove, Ill.: InterVarsity Press, 1998), 13.

for them and what songs bring God's grace to their lives), the hope is that the newcomers will eventually find meaning and inspiration in the traditional songs of the church they have chosen to join. The congregation invites others to learn and join in *their* story.

This model maintains and respects the musical history and tradition of the majority culture and expects persons from other cultures to start anew in finding meaningful inspiration through different musical forms and styles. Theologically, this affirms the way God has been mediated through the dominant culture but ignores or denies the way God has been experienced and incarnated in other cultures. In reality, it boxes God into a particular cultural framework. It can also create a dichotomy in the minds and hearts of those from other cultures. The God of their cultural past is brought out at home during the week in private or family devotionals while the God of their corporate worship is the same God but accessed in potentially new and unfamiliar ways in Sunday worship. The burden of learning new music is placed on the newcomers.

(2) A second model attempts to treat everyone equally by using music that is initially new to all cultures. New, contemporary music is used. In many ways this model denies the traditions and histories of everyone in order for each to start out anew creating a shared memory through music. Congregational hymnody is often composed of repetitive praise choruses. The praise choruses are easy to learn and they don't require great fluency in the English language. *Coritos* (similar to praise choruses in that they are short and repetitive) are very popular in Hispanic churches where various cultures come together, united by the Spanish language. There are many hymns composed in Spanish, but a person from Mexico may not know the hymnody of Argentina or Puerto Rico or Guatemala or Spain. *Coritos* are easy to learn and are often accompanied by guitars and other native instruments.

This model does attempt to treat everyone equally—not just from every culture but also the unchurched who have no faith history or musical traditions. The praise choruses of contemporary Christian music that have been composed by European American artists are based on a pop culture that is Western in tonality. And since the music doesn't resonate with the past, it takes awhile for persons not only to learn the music but to appropriate it for their spiritual expression in worship, to use it as a means of truly praising God and as a means of experiencing God's presence.

Theologically, this model of music in worship keeps God in the present—focused on the musical genre of contemporary pop culture. While the lyrics are often scripturally based, it is usually one phrase of scripture that is repeated rather than an interpretation of a particular text or pericope. The lyrics also describe a God who is wholly other–a transcendent God. In multiethnic congregations, however (and I would argue, in all multicultural congregations), it is important for the immanent nature of God to be proclaimed as well. Until we can see the face of God in the "other," in those who are truly different than we are, racism and prejudice will continue to run rampant in our church and society.

The lyrics and musical composition of praise choruses are usually limited in nature. The music is used to create a feeling or mood among the participants, but the lyrics don't challenge one's intellectual side, nor do they usually deal with the rich metaphorical language of the Christian faith that allows for the multivalent possibilities of expression and interpretation. Obviously, these are broad, general statements and much depends on the music and lyrics that are used. Many of the lyrics are also personal in nature, using "I" language that deals with one's individual relationship to God. For corporate worship, especially in multicultural congregations, the collective "we" language is important for developing the shared story. Because much of this music is "praise choruses," the lyrics focus on the vertical dimension of worship. Care needs to be taken so that the songs chosen, or lyrics written, also address the horizontal or discipleship aspects of worship. Servanthood should not be left out of our corporate worship.

While this model focuses on the present, the deep, abiding sense of God's presence through history and tradition seems lacking when the music of everyone's past is discarded in search of a common present. The various limitations of the musical style and lyrics of praise choruses can imply a limited dimension of our role as disciples in God's kin-dom and can unintentionally offer a limited understanding of the great and mysterious God we serve.

(3) Another model attempts to find the common bond that exists between the diverse members of the congregation. Some congregations have chosen to identify which hymn tunes the various cultures have in common. Is there any shared story, any shared memory through hymnody? Are there some songs that the majority of the congregation finds meaningful to use in honoring and praising God; any hymns that mediate God's grace to everyone's lives?

For good or ill, missionaries took Western hymnody with them around the world. Many of our nineteenth-century hymns are sung by persons of other cultures in a variety of languages. In some cases, the lyrics are the same (interpreted into other languages). In other hymns, however, the tune is the same, but the lyrics are different. The Korean hymnal, for example, has the "Ode to Joy" tune in it with beautiful lyrics appropriate for a wedding. Other hymns have the same lyrics (loosely translated), but other problems may arise for today's multicultural congregations.

One problem is that while those songs were sung many years ago, in some denominations in this country, they have moved out of the mainstream of congregational hymnody. New hymnals have been published; new hymns have been introduced and accepted into the life of the congregation. The "old" songs may still have deep meaning for older generations as they offer praise to God and receive grace, but for others, these songs may be totally unfamiliar or may not play the same role in one's vertical relationship with God during worship.

In other churches, the problem lies with the theology that undergirds the lyrics of the nineteenth-century missionary hymns. The theology and imagery don't always speak to the church today. Hymns with pastoral (field and pasture) images don't have the same meaning in an inner-city community surrounded by cement. Communion hymns that stress atonement for personal sins don't facilitate a theology of celebration of the sacrament where the diverse people of God gather around the banquet table.

If model two tends to exist in the present, this model in its extreme tends to remain fixed in the past. It is an attempt at finding a shared memory as it values the histories of each of the cultures represented in the congregation. It also asserts the enduring presence of God in our past. But it limits God to the testimonies (through the written lyrics) of authors written decades ago, and the hymn tunes and rhythms remain Western in nature. It's a theology of God mediated through Western European and European American culture. This is not to deny that those hymns have deep meaning for Christians from other cultures. In their conversion experience, those hymns may be foundational to their faith journeys. But theologically, it still keeps God boxed in a past time and culture.

(4) The last model best describes culturally-conscious worship. In this model, the congregation's music is meaningful to the various members of the church regardless of what culture they come from. The diverse ways that people of every culture offer praise to God and receive inspiration from God through music are welcomed into the worship of the multicultural congregation. Throughout the Christian year, this often results in a variety of musical forms and styles, but it exposes everyone to the music (and possibly language) that honors God and facilitates experiencing the presence of God for different individuals and cultural communities.

I realize that blending musical forms feels unharmonious to some, and the choice of which music goes where in the service sometimes feels haphazard. Blending musical forms can create much resistance from longtime members of the congregation. That's where the testimony or the shared story is crucial. If we are truly to be a community for one another, it is important that we hear the testimony of the one(s) for whom this music is foundational in their praise to God, how this music facilitates the vertical aspect of worship for them. It is a gift to have someone share the personal meaning of a particular song or how his or her faith has been deepened by a particular hymn. In honor and support of that person's faith journey and presence in the body of Christ (facilitating the horizontal aspect of worship), that song (maybe a totally unfamiliar song) takes on new meaning for the entire congregation. (This issue will be dealt with in more detail in the "Musical Testimony" section.)

Granted, eliciting this testimony from members of the congregation from other cultures may be difficult given the cultural complexities described in the previous chapter, yet to be a truly welcoming community, it is important to know what forms of liturgy and what music were and are foundational to their worship experience.

Where there are hymn tunes in common, they may be incorporated with their original lyrics (and respective translations) or alternative words may be used. There are many new lyrics today (sung to traditional hymn tunes) that address the issues and spirituality of multicultural congregations. This allows for a common history (through the tune) and a new start for all (through the lyrics).[12] (Appendix C provides a list of many of these hymns found in mainline Protestant hymnals.)

In many ways the principle of this model is the same as the assimilation model, except it is reciprocal. The assimilation model hopes (sometimes assumes) that the music of the majority culture will become a means for those of other cultures to also access God. In this fourth model, this hope is reciprocal. It is also desired that the music of the minority cultures will become another exciting means for those of the majority culture to access God. This model keeps all parishioners rooted in their individual and/or cultural past faith

---

[12]Doran and Troeger in *Trouble at the Table: Gathering The Tribes for Worship* (Nashville: Abingdon Press, 1992) argue that the use of new lyrics to familiar tunes combines structure and antistructure simultaneously, and "the conflicting messages cancel the potential strength of either element" (p. 99). I disagree. Not only is this practice an integral part of the history of Christian hymnody (hymn writers often used the familiar tunes of the culture to accompany their Christian lyrics), but I also believe that the familiar tunes keep us rooted in a sense of God's abiding presence in our past while the new lyrics open us up for new revelations of God's acting in our present context while guiding us toward the future kin-dom vision.

journeys with God, but God's presence in our lives is not left in the past. By learning the inspirational music of other cultures, this model offers unlimited future possibilities for experiencing God anew while creating shared stories and shared memories in the present. (Appendix B provides a list of music from other cultures that is included in many mainline Protestant hymnals.) Theologically, it proclaims a God who is not boxed in or limited by any culture or time period but who delights in a multitude of avenues of praise and who reciprocates blessing and grace through even more unexpected avenues to our hearts.

In Psalm 137 the Hebrew people have been taken captive and are living in Babylon. There they sit down and weep: "How could we sing the Lord's song in a foreign land?" (v. 4). Sometimes I wonder if new immigrants to this country find it difficult to "sing the Lord's song [as they know it] in a foreign land." For this reason, many choose homogenous congregations composed primarily of persons from their native land where the songs they sing are not viewed as "inappropriate" or "odd" for Christian worship. Others join a multicultural congregation that has separate worship services for different language ministries: separate services conducted in Spanish, Korean, or Tagalog. I believe, however, that multicultural congregations can also provide avenues whereby persons born in other countries can "sing the Lord's song in a foreign land."

Eliciting the Vertical Stories

In order to create a shared story within multicultural congregations, it is important to find ways to elicit the individual and collective cultural stories of the diverse persons present in the congregations.

Visitation

As in any congregation, pastoral or lay visitation in people's homes is a great way to develop a relationship with newcomers. During home visitations, the pastor and laypersons can get to know the persons on a deeper level; they can observe the visual symbols of the home environment; they can ask, "Is it well with your soul?" Through visitation, the pastor or laypersons can also elicit what worship was like when they were growing up or what worship was like in their native country, what elements of worship are particularly meaningful for them, what music best offers praise to God from their culture, and what kind of prayers best express the depths of their souls.

Culturally, keep in mind two things. First, if the persons being visited are new to this country and are from hierarchically oriented, "shame-based" or "face-saving" cultures, the pastor's questions may be answered with indirect responses in order not to appear to be criticizing the current worship style that is led by the pastor. Critique would bring shame on the pastor as well as on the persons offering the critique. Lay visitors (who are of the same status as the persons being visited) may be able to more accurately elicit the meaningful vertical and horizontal aspects of worship.

One pastor of a multicultural congregation has developed a questionnaire that he uses as preparation for his home visitations when he is trying to learn what vertical aspects of worship were foundational for his parishioners in their home countries or native cultures. (This questionnaire is included in appendix D to stimulate your own ways to elicit this information.)

The second issue to keep in mind is that cultural orientations to time also have an effect on visitations. In cultures like the United States that are monochronic in their time orientation, pastors often call ahead and make an appointment to visit someone. Dropping by unannounced may be perceived as an imposition, or as being rude or inconsiderate. However, in other cultures, making an appointment may be perceived as "keeping your distance," wanting a more formal (rather than informal or intimate) relationship. Stopping by for a visit (even at mealtimes) is perfectly acceptable to some and may imply a deep desire to really develop a relationship with this person.[13]

Musical Testimonies

Eliciting the vertical stories can also be facilitated by musical testimonies, which can take a variety of forms. An individual can testify to the importance of a particular song on her or his faith journey. In some congregations it would be appropriate for this testimony to be in verbal storytelling form immediately before the hymn is sung. However, in more formal congregations, this testimony may be shared verbally before the service begins in an announcement time (although in some multicultural congregations one-fourth to one-half of the congregation may show up after the service begins), or the testimony can be printed in the bulletin.

One Mexican American woman shared with a multicultural congregation how important the hymn "*Jesus es mi Rey Soberano*" ("O Jesus, my King and my Sovereign") was to her cultural community and to her personal faith journey. While the tune and lyrics were

---

[13]Elmer, 14.

initially unfamiliar to many in the congregation, this hymn (sung in Spanish and English) has been added to the congregation's hymnody and is sung periodically throughout the year. Or the congregation could learn the hymn of the Independent Church of South Africa, "*Amen Siakudumisa*" ("Amen, we praise your name, O Lord"), which was sung "at the enthronement of Desmond Tutu as Archbishop of Capetown."[14] As the throng of people sang this song, Tutu began to move in time to the music. For the black South Africans, "this was a great sign that their music and culture was being recognised as integral to the worship of God."[15]

In learning new music, some people accept it more readily when the horizontal connection is made with specific individuals for whom this music is spiritually enriching; hence the personal story sharing. The Reverend Marcelle Dotson, pastor of Greenwood Memorial United Methodist Church in Dorchester, Massachusetts, shares the following story of a musical testimony offered in their church.

> What is understood in our congregation is that during the "Prayers of the Peolple," members are free to suggest a hymn for all to sing, to lead us in one of the island choruses, or to share a solo which has particular meaning for them. One of the most moving experiences of this type of prayer was when one of our more quiet members shared a very powerful and emotional song of thanks to God. She's from Honduras and the song was in Spanish. That did not matter. The faith and emotion behind the song were so evident that it brought chillls even to those who did not know the language.[16]

It would seem to me that eventually culturally-conscious worship would be able to embrace music from other cultures simply because it is part of the vertical relationship to God in the worship of Christians from those cultures. Many persons who are not African American sing "Lift Every Voice and Sing" to remember the horrors of slavery and to celebrate the faith and hope of the African American community. But that song has also touched the souls of persons who are not of that community because of their own hardships and struggles.

---

[14]John L. Bell, ed., *Many and Great: Songs of the World Church* (Glasgow, Scotland: Wild Goose Publications of the Iona Community, 1990), 49.

[15]Ibid.

[16]Taken from the "Multi-ethnic New Circular," an internet newsletter of the United Methodist Church for multiethnic congregations, February 10, 2000. To get on their list, send your e-mail address to Douglas Ruffle at DRuffle@gbgm-umc.org.

I realize that in this global community, elements from various cultures are constantly being borrowed and shared. Care does need to be taken, however, so we do not abuse or misappropriate the symbols, music, or arts of another culture for our own personal gain while ignoring the communities from which they come (e.g., using sign language to accompany a song when the rest of the service is not interpreted for persons who are deaf, and the church has no intention of starting a deaf ministry). Using music from other cultures should be done with respect and active solidarity. When done appropriately, embracing Christian music worldwide opens up rich alternative spheres of praising God for everyone, expands our notions of God, and allows Christians from every culture to hold one another in respect and tender care.

When new music is introduced to the congregation, the World Council of Churches recommends the use of an "animator." The animator is the one who knows the song the best–its nuances, rhythm, tone, tempo. The animator helps the congregation learn the total *feel* of the song–not just the lyrics, tune, and tempo. To appropriate a song into one's spiritual life, the song needs to be felt. It's not a matter of simply learning the words and tune. If the song is to be sung in its native language, the animator teaches the congregation the pronunciation of the words and how the words work together to create the appropriate rhythm.

Artistic Testimonies

Another form of musical testimony is the use of the various instruments, dance, and dramatic arts that are used in worship throughout the world. In some countries in Africa, the drum beat is considered to be the heartbeat of the community. People bring their entire bodies to the dance of life accompanied by the heartbeat of the drums. In Tonga, there is an instrument called the *lali*. It is a hollowed-out piece of wood that is hit with a mallet. Before the Christians arrived in the islands, the *lali* was used to call people to worship or to a community gathering. Culturally, the *lali* was used to announce that the king had a message to give to the people. It can be used in Christian worship to signal the beginning of worship: Come, God has a message for the people.

Biblical and contemporary dramas are being utilized in some multicultural congregations. When choosing persons to participate in biblical dramas, it is important to include persons from a wide variety of cultures so that Jesus or the disciples are not always played by persons of the majority culture.

Contemporary dramas often deal with issues people struggle with today. It's important to get diverse input into the creation of these dramas because the issues persons from various cultures face and need God's wisdom for vary greatly. The concerns of upper middle-class European Americans are different from the struggles of Native Americans living on and off their tribal lands. The concerns of undocumented immigrants are worlds apart from third-generation immigrants to this country. The themes of contemporary dramas should deal with the wide range of issues faced by the various cultures and generations in the congregation.

One multicultural congregation outside Washington, D.C., has a chancel choir (consisting predominantly of European American members, but also some African and Caribbean members), a gospel choir (with mostly African and Caribbean members but with some European American members), a liturgical dance group, an African dance group, an African drumming group, and a steel drum group that plays music from the Caribbean. Though initially these groups were started by those from the cultures that the art forms represent, over time, as youth and adults become involved, these dance and drum groups will be composed of diverse groups of people offering musical testimonies spiritually enriching to all.

Keep in mind, however, that dancing (of any kind) may not be acceptable in the worship of certain denominations in certain cultures because the missionaries associated the traditional cultural dances with non-Christian religions. These dances continue to exist in the life of the cultural community, but not on Sundays during worship. While the Roman Catholics in the South Pacific have rich dance traditions during Sunday worship services, Methodists in the islands usually forbid any dance on Sundays. Korea also has rich dance traditions within its culture, but dance is not appropriate during Sunday worship.

Sharing the Horizontal Stories
Sharing One's Culture

While it is crucial for the vertical aspects of worship to be carefully fostered during the design and leading of worship, the horizontal aspect of worship cannot be ignored–especially in multicultural congregations. The cultural complexities raised in the previous chapter show how important it is for the people to get to know one another on more than a surface level. Various opportunities outside the liturgy and during worship itself can nurture the horizontal aspects of worship and can foster a shared story.

Educational Opportunities

Some of the cultural complexities raised in the last chapter may need to be discussed and explored in places other than worship, although the Children's Time may be a place to learn about our differences and celebrate them as creations of God. Other educational and fellowship opportunities in the life of the congregation can also help identify possible conflicts that arise from hidden or primary culture rather than surface culture.

Sharing the Bible

One particularly important way persons can share their culture with others is through participating in Bible studies. While we all share a basic common story of God's saving acts in history, the life, ministry, death, and resurrection of Jesus, and God's kin-dom visions for the future, this story has been mediated through various cultural lenses. It is fascinating to hear how these biblical texts are interpreted by persons of other cultures.

Greetings

Early Christians greeted one another with the "holy kiss" of peace. Kissing someone who is not family or an intimate friend is uncomfortable for many European Americans. It's not part of the culture. We prefer a hug (for those we know well) or a handshake (for those less familiar to us). So in most European American congregations, we have adapted the ancient "holy kiss" into something more acceptable to this culture. Other cultures have likewise adapted the "holy kiss" of the early Christians and greet one another in more culturally appropriate ways.

In several multicultural congregations, various members teach how people greet each other in their particular culture. This not only alleviates the "greeting" confusions that can occur in multicultural congregations (discussed in chapter 3), but it also fosters the horizontal aspect of worship. In one congregation, right before the Passing of the Peace, a member of the congregation demonstrates the appropriate way to greet people in his or her culture (Filipino "mano pa," or African handshake, or Indonesian style of greeting, or a handshake, or a kiss on each cheek). The people are then asked to greet each other with that particular greeting during the Passing of the Peace.

Another congregation uses verbal greetings in other languages rather than the gestural form of greeting. One of the laity teaches the congregation how to say "Hello" or "The peace of God be with you" in her or his native language. The people then greet one another in this new tongue. This manner of Passing God's Peace through various forms of greeting reinforces that God's incarnating acts are not limited to any one culture and that we can greet one another with God's peace in many ways.

The same greeting (gestural or verbal) may be used for several weeks in a row (so people really remember it), or a different greeting may be taught the following Sunday. The various greetings could also be taught during a Children's Time, inviting the children to share that greeting with members of the congregation.

Another congregation invites the lay liturgists and lay scripture readers to greet the congregation in their native languages prior to reading the scripture or as they introduce themselves at the beginning of worship.

Sharing God's Peace

Many multicultural congregations have found the Passing of the Peace to be meaningful whether cultural forms of greeting are shared in conjunction with the Peace or not. For some congregations, this liturgical element is known as a time of fellowship or friendship. It is a time where the people greet one another. I have heard several stories from pastors of multicultural congregations who feel this element in the worship service lasts way too long. People leave their seats and move into the aisles to greet many people—not just those sitting next to, in front of, or behind them. In smaller congregations (a hundred or less), it seems as if everyone has to greet everyone else before the service can continue.

While it may take up extra time in the worship service, this is an important part of the horizontal aspect of worship, and in multicultural congregations, horizontal relationships need to be fostered among such diverse members. When this time in the worship service is more than just "hello," but is some form of liturgical greeting, as in "the peace of God be with you," this element of worship facilitates the horizontal and vertical aspects of worship as we become mediators of God's grace to one another.

Sharing One's Joys and Concerns

Some form of the Prayers of the People is also common in multicultural congregations that are not too large. Many congregations phrase it as "Joys and Concerns" or "Celebrations and Prayer Requests." However it is named, it is an important part of worship that, like the Passing of the Peace, facilitates the horizontal aspects of worship. People share how God has blessed them, and they ask for the community's prayers for themselves and their loved ones here and back "home," wherever that may be.

But people also move beyond their own insulated worlds and offer prayers for the larger community: the gangs in the neighborhood, the mothers living on the streets with their children because they have no place to call home, those who have lost loved ones in natural disasters, the rebuilding after wars, the children orphaned as a result of war. During this prayer time, the world is brought into the sanctuary, and the people take these prayer requests with them as they leave the sanctuary to continue the horizontal aspects of worship in their daily lives, to be disciples of God's love in the world.

Sharing One's Faith Journey

Testimonials, or the sharing of one's faith journey, are still used in many denominations. Some are including testimony during Friday evening services or Wednesday night prayer meetings. Sharing faith journeys during worship is another way to introduce people to one another, to learn about Christianity in other cultures, and to foster both the horizontal and vertical aspects of worship. As the person shares with the congregation how God has moved in her or his life, the congregation gets in touch with God's presence in the lives of the other members and becomes inspired by the faith journey of the other.

Summary

There are many ways a congregation can elicit and share the faith stories of the diverse members of the congregation. Held in common, these stories create a shared memory and contribute to friendship and trust. But sharing our stories also fosters the development of the new culture that is emerging, a culture that is a blending of the rich heritages of all.

The stories may tell of the pain of being homesick for one's native land, culture, and church, or the stories may share one's urgent desire to learn about and fit into the American culture and a local church as quickly and effectively as possible. Learning about the other fosters a recognition of the other without falling into preconceived notions that lead to stereotyping. Whatever the stories express, they allow diverse persons to form a true community, supportive of one another.

CHAPTER FIVE

Culturally-Conscious Worship: Balancing and Blending

Whenever more than one culture worships together, there is the possibility of conflicting expectations and needs. It is possible (and common) to force one group to do all the compromising, but culturally-conscious worship works at negotiating these differences through balancing and blending the stories of our lives with worship's larger story.

Balancing the Vertical and Horizontal

Both eliciting and sharing the stories that people bring with them to the worship experience helps maintain a balance between the horizontal and vertical aspects of worship. Focus on the vertical aspects of worship gives God praise and honor and brings inspiration and empowerment to our lives as we experience God's unconditional love and abiding presence. Fostering the horizontal aspects of worship can certainly break down cultural barriers that divide us and can create a strong social network and hopefully a strong justice outreach ministry into the community.

But a balance needs to be kept between these two dimensions. On the one hand, if we focus solely on the vertical relationship, people can get caught up in a "me and God" mentality that overshadows relationships to others and our environment. Coming to church and feeling good and lifted up, focusing on one's vertical relationship to

God, can be rewarding for recent immigrants struggling to adapt to their new country, for persons under the poverty line struggling to survive, for persons who feel on the margins of society and struggle for acceptance and validation. So much of life feels hard, even desperate. Participating in an alternative reality in worship where one knows she or he is important to God gives people the strength and confidence to continue to confront the injustices in the world. But focusing only on oneself and one's needs can block out the need for our discipleship in the world. On the other hand, if we focus solely on the horizontal relationship of worship, the church can turn into another social service club.

The balance between these two aspects of worship and, most importantly, the innate connection between the two is crucial to culturally-conscious worship. The horizontal dimensions of worship are undergirded and informed by the vertical dimension, and the vertical relationship is lived out in the horizontal plane. They are intimately tied to one another.

Balancing Visual Symbols

Balancing the vertical and horizontal aspects of worship can also be facilitated through visual symbols. Most churches have the vertical symbols: the cross (symbol of God's incarnation in Jesus and God's power over death), the Bible (symbol of God's word and the testimonies of the faithful), candles (symbol of Jesus as the light of the world–except in many Haitian congregations where candles are associated with voodoo worship), flowers or greenery (symbol of God's beauty in creation), baptismal font and water (symbol of initiation into the family of God, the body of Christ), and altar/table and communion elements (symbol of God's presence with us, in us, and among us).

Horizontal images may include the American flag and Christian flag that are found in many churches in this country. In multicultural congregations, the flags (symbols of God's presence and saving acts in nations around the globe) of the other countries represented in the congregation can also be displayed. Altar cloths made from traditional fabrics of other cultures (symbols of the gifts of the land and the labor and imaginations of the people) can be rotated throughout the Christian year. Some clergy wear a bright, colorful stole made in Guatemala or made from African kente cloth. Several multicultural congregations also have choir "stoles" made out of kente cloth. Banners can depict the languages or cultures represented in the congregation. If one walks into a multicultural congregation, will one know that it is multicultural by the visual environment?

Visuals can also be used to communicate in powerful ways. What colors, symbols, and images are used in the various native cultures to honor the preparation periods of Advent or Lent? How are Christmas and Easter celebrated? What visuals will make these grand celebrations in the life of the church come alive for the diverse people present?

Balancing the Comfortable and the Unsettling

Most multicultural congregations began as a homogenous community. The people were comfortable with one another–they shared a common culture and history. Regardless of the motivations for becoming multicultural, the presence of "the other" in their midst is somewhat unsettling. Becoming multicultural has necessitated many changes in attitude, theology, and leadership. What has always been comfortable is challenged often as the congregation becomes multicultural. Changing worship creates even more uncertainty. Holding on to the comforting traditions of worship is, in many ways, the cornerstone that keeps the original members steady in the midst of change. So an assimilation form of worship is easy to understand. It is familiar and controllable.

But what is the experience of newer members? If they are recent immigrants, there may be very little that feels comfortable or familiar. Being a minority person in the midst of the majority culture can also be unsettling. If we are to let go of total control and let God enter our lives in unexpected ways, it is important that culturally-conscious worship keep a balance for everyone between the comforting and the unsettling.

This is important for all worship, not just for multicultural worship. If nothing is unsettling, if nothing forces us out of the familiar, if there is no room for the unexpected, then there is also no room for mystery and therefore no room for God or the Holy Spirit to work in our lives. Change is unsettling; letting go is often unsettling. But it is often in these experiences that we make room for the Divine to enter our lives.

In multicultural congregations, however, what is comforting to some may be unsettling to others. For example, being caught up in the emotion of the Spirit working amid the congregants is very familiar to persons from some ethnic and denominational cultures. Spirit mediums or shamans are common, so experiencing someone (or oneself) physically and emotionally being "caught up in the Spirit's power" is not only acceptable, it may be expected. But persons from cultures where this is not common may experience discomfort in the presence of such practice.

Likewise, the recitation of a creed may be comforting to many in European American Protestant congregations; they may expect a creed to be included in every worship service. But Protestants from cultures that associate creeds with Roman Catholicism may experience the recitation of a creed as unfamiliar and unsettling.

Identifying what is comforting to those from other cultures is important so that the design, content, and style of worship can provide a balance whereby both the comforting and the unsettling is present for *all*. Doran and Troeger talk about this dynamic as maintaining a balance between structure and antistructure. Structure is those aspects of worship that facilitate "assurance, order, clear definition, dependability, things under control,"[1] and antistructure is those elements (silence, symbol, Spirit, ambiguity, insight, feeling) that are "more elusive, mysterious, and uncontrolled."[2] But as we have already noted, in multiethnic congregations, what is ordered and controllable for some is elusive and uncontrollable for others.

They also argue that there needs to be a balance between intra-dependence and extra-dependence in worship. Intra-dependence is "the state of depending upon ourselves," while extra-dependence is the state of depending upon another.[3] Worship that is solely intra-dependent is tightly controlled but leaves no room for unsettling times where the Spirit can move and the Divine can enter. But worship that is solely extra-dependent can put us in a position of never taking responsibility for making changes in our own lives or for alleviating the unjust conditions in our world.[4] Worship needs a balance, a moving "back and forth between intra-dependence and extra-dependence."[5]

Balancing Precatechesis and Catechesis

Many congregations today who are doing intentional evangelism and outreach programs into the unchurched community are providing worship experiences that introduce persons who are seeking a form of spirituality for their lives (known as seekers) to the Christian faith. *Precatechesis* refers to this learning stage of Christian formation. An

---

[1]Carol Doran and Thomas H. Troeger, *Trouble at the Table: Gathering the Tribes for Worship* (Nashville: Abingdon Press, 1992), 94.

[2]Ibid., 95–96.

[3]Ibid., 101.

[4]Ibid., 102.

[5]Ibid., 101.

outsider approaches the Christian culture to ascertain if there is any spiritual fulfillment to be obtained there.[6]

There are some worship services aimed at seekers where the liturgy is designed to be comfortable and inoffensive to those who have little or no church background. It is hoped that worship is truly visitor friendly. Since the purpose is to get seekers in the door of the church, provide a nonthreatening visual and verbal environment, and move them to a belief in God and Jesus Christ, some congregations design the liturgy so the seekers don't have to participate. They are not asked to stand and introduce themselves or to contribute to the offering plate. Neither must they listen to religious vocabulary that is for "insiders" only. A worship service designed solely for those in this seeker stage also tends not to challenge persons for discipleship in the world. Discipleship comes later, after a commitment to Jesus Christ has been made. Andy Langford in *Transitions in Worship* identifies performance-oriented worship (influenced by aesthetics and the enlightenment) and entertainment-oriented worship (influenced by pop culture) that are often used in targeting this seeker population. The traditional style of worship that focuses on participation may seem too threatening to this population.[7]

A participatory style of worship is more common among long-term believers. *Catechesis* refers to the spiritual formation of Christians on their faith journeys. It is in-depth study, covenanting with other Christians, active discipleship, and spiritual empowerment for acts of justice, mercy, and kindness in the world. Worship for catechetical purposes assumes a basic common belief in God, Jesus Christ, and the Holy Spirit, an understanding of the stories and characters of the Bible, and a shared religious vocabulary. Worship deepens our faith, expands our knowledge of the Bible and the faithful witnesses throughout history, and challenges us to share God's love with others.

Multicultural congregations, like any other congregation that does intentional evangelism, will be faced with the need to balance precatechesis and catechesis. There will be members of the congregation who are deeply formed Christians and non-Christians who (in immigrant communities) may come to the church for English as a Second Language class and decide to come to worship. A balance

---

[6]Daniel Benedict and Craig Kennet Miller, *Contemporary Worship for the 21st Century: Worship or Evangelism?* (Nashville: Discipleship Resources of the United Methodist Church, 1994), 43.

[7]Andy Langford, *Transitions in Worship: Moving from Traditional to Contemporary* (Nashville: Abingdon Press, 1999), 128–30.

will need to be kept so that the seekers feel accepted while the faithful Christians are challenged to develop their spirituality to even greater depths.

Multicultural congregations, however, present another conversation in the discussion of precatechesis and catechesis. The assumed shared religious vocabulary may become skewed in the translation from one language to another, and the interpretation of theological concepts and biblical texts may not be held in common. So while each of us may be deeply committed Christians in our native culture, we may feel like neophytes in the presence of the cultural and religious practices of another. In some ways, in culturally-conscious worship, if we take seriously the various cultures among us, we are all in some sort of precatechetical stage, a learning process, in relationship to the cultures and religious practices different from our own. We are all in a catechetical stage in relationship to deepening our understanding of our own culture and religious practices. In a European American congregation with a large percentage of persons from the islands of Tonga, the Tongans are precatechetical in their understanding of American culture and the European Americans are pre-catechetical in their learning of Tongan culture. But through the interaction of the two cultures, we come to know the rich spiritualities present. We also become aware of our own culture and begin to see how it has influenced our religious practices. Our spirituality grows and deepens as we interact with persons of another culture.

Blending Older Generations and Younger Generations

Many multicultural congregations have found that it is exceptionally important to include the younger generations as much as possible in the life of the church—including worship. In many European American congregations, children are often not present for the entire worship service. In some congregations, Sunday school is held at the same time as worship, and children seldom attend worship at all. In other congregations, the children stay for the first ten to fifteen minutes of worship and then go to either Sunday school or to "junior church." Junior church is an attempt to meet the children on their educational level, but in many congregations, junior church is not "worship" but rather more lessons and crafts, biblical videos, and other activities. The children may have a strong religious education, but they have little or no spiritual touchstone with worship. This is not true in Korean congregations. The English language ministries for children, youth, and young adults are often separate from the Korean-speaking worship service, but when the English language ministries meet, they usually have a full worship service that is age appropriate.

Having Sunday school for children during worship or sending children to junior church is not common in other cultures. It is important for the children to be present in worship to be socialized and inculturated into the hymnody, prayers, symbols, preaching, and postures of worship.

In many multicultural congregations, children and youth are encouraged to develop confidence in leadership by participating in choir or dance troupes, drumming groups, or bell choirs. But they are also asked to be scripture readers, ushers, and acolytes, and to lead other aspects of the liturgy.

Developing a sense of confidence in oneself and one's abilities is extremely helpful to today's youth, but it is equally important to assist them in developing the cross-cultural communication and social skills that are necessary in our multicultural world. As these skills are nurtured and developed in the Christian environment of a multicultural church, they are put into practice in the volatile atmospheres of many of our schools. The leadership learned in church is carried over into leadership roles and bridge-building roles between students of various cultures at school.

Blending Options for Culturally-Conscious Worship

Whenever persons from diverse cultures worship together, there are often different expectations regarding worship practice. After the faith stories and "liturgical homeland" stories have been shared, multiple blending options become available.

For those in denominations who have a common liturgy through a "prayer book," one might want to consider a diversity of musical forms and styles, alternative artistic offerings, and multicultural interpretations of the lectionary texts in preaching.

For those from more "free church" traditions, consider also balancing other liturgical elements according to the "liturgical homelands" of the people in the congregation: Calls to Worship (proclamation of a Psalm text, responsive greeting in contemporary language, opening prayer, greeting, etc.), prayer forms (printed corporate prayers, extemporaneous prayers, prayers led by a layperson, prayers led by the pastor(s), prayers written by persons from other countries, Korean Tong Song Kido prayer form, etc.), and prayer postures (sitting, standing, kneeling).

There is also the possibility of alternating creeds and affirmations of faith from different cultures and time periods (using the Apostles'

Creed, Korean Creed, affirmation of faith from the United Church of Canada, etc.) or using cultural adaptations of the Lord's Prayer (a Maori version from the New Zealand Book of Common Prayer,[8] a Nicaraguan version,[9] or the Lord's Prayer written by the Council of American Indian Ministries[10]).

In terms of sacramental practices, some cultures are accustomed to baptism through immersion, while others prefer sprinkling, and still others pouring. In several denominations today, all three modes of baptism are possible. Those from Vietnam can be baptized through immersion, while European Americans can be sprinkled, and water can be poured from a seashell over the head of a Native American infant.

Communion practices also vary from culture to culture. Some partake of the communion elements (bread and wine or grape juice) by kneeling at the altar and taking first the bread and then the cup. Others partake of the communion elements while sitting in their seats. Still others take both elements simultaneously as they dip the bread in the cup using the method of intinction. Receiving communion through intinction is often done while standing, but it can also be used in a sitting or kneeling posture.

The communion elements can also be varied. Some cultures or denominations use wafers, others use small cubes of cut up bread, and still others use a whole loaf of bread. In some cultures that don't grow wheat or grapes, where bread and wine products are very expensive, the staple food of the country may be used in place of bread: tortillas, rice cakes, Native American fry bread, Indian roti or naan–any food that is the "staff of life" for the people. The use of grape juice and wine also varies. Throughout the Christian year, consider changing the postures of communion, the form of receiving, and the elements used to allow persons from various cultures to feel "at home" with the sacrament. Kneeling may be appropriate for the Lenten season in preparation for the passion and death of Jesus. Standing is the posture of celebration and could be used during the Easter season. Sitting may be appropriate for the ordinary times between Epiphany and Lent, and between the Day of Pentecost and Advent.

Given such diverse possibilities of blending various aspects of the liturgy, it is important to try to identify a common theme, textual

---

[8]Anglican Church of New Zealand, *A New Zealand Prayer Book* (Auckland: William Collins Publishers, 1989), 181.

[9]Maren C. Tirabassi and Kathy Wonson Eddy, *Gifts of Many Cultures* (Cleveland: United Church Press, 1995), 49.

[10]Ibid., 48.

image, topic, sacramental occasion, or cultural focus that will be the guiding force for the decision making for any given Sunday. Without some cord that binds the diverse elements together, culturally-conscious worship can feel scattered and diffuse. Great care and intentionality has to be given to every aspect of the service.

Think through the content and tone of voice for the opening of the service. What tone is being set from the beginning? How are mood shifts handled? How does one go from an uplifting, strong, corporate hymn of celebration to a meditative time of prayer? If the sermon precedes the closing hymn and is challenging and necessitates reflection, what transition is necessary for the congregation to move from a reflective posture to a corporate affirmation of their commitment to discipleship in a closing hymn of dedication? How much verbal instruction is needed to guide people from one aspect of the liturgy to another? When is verbal instruction intrusive and interruptive, and when is it being visitor friendly for the newer members of the congregation? Can instructions for sitting and standing be given through gestures rather than verbally (take care, however, if you have persons in the congregation who are blind)? How will stories be shared from the various cultures to introduce new music or to teach a particular gesture of greeting or to give a testimony of one's faith? These stories can be woven into the liturgy in such a way that it doesn't function as an "aside" or as an interruption to the service, but it does require some preplanning and consultation with those sharing their stories.

In many ways, designing worship is like a work of art, a carefully choreographed dance or a well-directed play. We don't want to over-choreograph so that there is no room for the movement of the Spirit during the service itself, but at the same time we want to be Spirit led as we prayerfully design the service and choose the various elements necessary to facilitate such a diverse group of people experiencing both the vertical and horizontal dimensions of worship.

Living with Different Stories Simultaneously

In extremely diverse multicultural congregations, is it possible to live with different stories simultaneously? Can we claim a unity in God through Jesus Christ in the midst of our diversity in regard to worship styles and preferences? Can we live with ambiguity rather than forced unison?

For example, can it become acceptable for some to sit for a prayer of confession while members from Southeast Asia choose to stand and others (raised Episcopalian) choose to kneel? Can some listen to the sermon in quiet while others participate in an animated call and response? Can some move their bodies and dance to the rhythms of the music while others feel more in touch with the sacred by planting their feet firmly in place? Can some sing in one language and others in another, or can the Lord's Prayer be said in a multitude of languages simultaneously? Can those who spiritually need to name God in inclusive language sing "Creator, Christ, and Holy Ghost" at the end of the Doxology while others are singing "Father, Son, and Holy Ghost" without having neighbors look at them judgmentally?

If we can live with different stories simultaneously, it allows for each person (regardless of one's cultural or denominational background) to access the vertical and horizontal aspects of worship in ways that make God's presence most alive for them.

The Next Step

If you're looking forward to the next chapter, which describes the "how-to" principles for negotiating the various cultural complexities while designing worship that is culturally conscious, maintaining a balance between the vertical and horizontal dimensions of worship, and seeking to create a common story, a shared memory among diverse peoples, look no further. I have left that chapter up to you to write.

I truly believe that the preparation process for designing worship as well as the form, content, and style of the worship service itself will be as diverse as the various multicultural congregations found in the numerous denominations throughout this country. And both the preparation and the final worship service will depend on the cultural makeup of the congregation, the gifts and skills of the professional staff and the laity, and the leadership of the pastor(s). Each multicultural congregation will develop its own shared story, its own new culture, and design its own culturally-conscious worship for their particular community of faith.

Gray's Story

Gray is a wonderful man who is eighty-eight years old. He has had numerous operations and lives with pain most of the time. His wife of fifty-three years died a few years ago, and he eventually had to sell their home and move into a retirement home in another state. I've known Gray for about twelve years and throughout those twelve years, every time I asked him how he was or how things were going, he would always respond, "Fantastic." He never had a tone of irony or sarcasm. He always said a courageous, confident, uplifting, "Fantastic!" In the midst of the pain and the many changes in his life,

Gray is still able to affirm that all is well or at least there is the desired hope, undergirded with faith, that all will be well.

Congregations that are becoming multicultural also experience change and even pain. Yet "fantastic!" can also be our Christian response as we affirm God's presence in this in-between time, in the midst of change, and believe that all is well or at least all will be well if we hold fast in faith to God's kin-dom vision.

In very powerful ways, multicultural congregations are prophetic witnesses to our world, taking the lead in creating community despite the tremendous diversity among us. They provide a beacon of hope not only for the church of the future but also for our society and world. By finding unity in the midst of diversity, multicultural congregations are creating peace by seeing all as kin in the family of God, by seeing the face of Christ in one another.

Appendix A
Global Resources

Music

African Songs of Worship. Geneva: World Council of Churches, 1986.

Alleluia Aotearoa: Hymns and Songs for all Churches. Christchurch, New Zealand: The New Zealand Hymnbook Trust, 1993.

Asian Institute for Liturgy and Music and the World Council of Churches. *Asian Songs of Worship.* Quezon City, Philippines: R. R. Yan Printing Press, 1988.

Bell, John L., and Graham Maule. *Enemy of Apathy.* Glasgow, Scotland: Wild Goose Publications of the Iona Community, 1988.

———. *Heaven Shall Not Wait.* Glasgow: Wild Goose Publications of the Iona Community, 1994.

———. *Love from Below.* Glasgow, Scotland: Wild Goose Publications of the Iona Community, 1989.

———. *When Grief is Raw: Songs for Times of Sorrow and Bereavement.* Glasgow: Wild Goose Publications of the Iona Community, 1997.

Berthier, Jacques. *Music from Taize: Responses, Litanies, Acclamations, Canons.* Vol. 1. Chicago: GIA Publications, 1981.

———. *Music from Taize: Responses, Litanies, Acclamations, Canons.* Vol. 2. Chicago: GIA Publications, 1984.

Cancoes de Rua. Piracicaba: Editora Unimep, 1992.

Cardoso, Ernesto Barros. *Whole Life, Holy Life.* Rio de Janeiro: Instituto de Estudos da Religiao, 1993.

Carol Our Christmas: A Book of New Zealand Carols. Raumati Beach, New Zealand: The New Zealand Hymnbook Trust, 1996. Order from P.O. Box 2011, Raumati Beach, NZ 6450.

Chi, Gabriel C. S., and L. G. McKinney. *New Songs of Praise.* Hong Kong: Baptist Press, 1973.

117

Colvin, Tom. *Come Let Us Walk This Road Together: 43 Songs from Africa.* Carol Stream, Ill.: Hope Publishing, 1997.

——. *Fill Us With Your Love: And Other Hymns from Africa.* Carol Stream, Ill.: Agape, 1983.

Doran, Carol, and Thomas H. Troeger. *New Hymns for the Lectionary: To Glorify the Maker's Name.* New York: Oxford University Press, 1986.

Harling, Per. *Worshipping Ecumenically.* Geneva: WCC Publications, 1995.

Hymns from the Four Winds: A Collection of Asian American Hymns. Nashville: Abingdon Press, 1983.

The Iona Community. *Many and Great: Songs of the World Church.* Glasgow: Wild Goose Publications of the Iona Community, 1990.

The Iona Community. *Sent by the Lord: Songs of the World Church.* Glasgow: Wild Goose Publications of the Iona Community, 1991.

Kyodan, Nihon Kirisuto. *Hymns of the Church.* Tokyo: Board of Publications, the United Church of Christ in Japan, 1963.

Loh, I-to. *New Songs of Asian Cities.* Taiwan: Urban and Industrial Mission Committee of the East Asian Christian Conference, 1972.

Mil Voces para Celebrar: Himnario Metodista. Nashville: United Methodist Publishing House, 1996.

New Songs of Asian Cities. Taiwan: Peng-cheng Printing, 1972. Order from Tainan Theological College, 115 East Gate Rd., Tainan, Taiwan ROC, or Christian Conference of Asia–UIM, 1-551-54 Totsuka, Shinjuku-ku, Tokyo 160 Japan.

One World Songs. London: Methodist World Development Action Campaign, 1978. Order from Methodist Church Division of Social Responsibility, 1 Central Buildings, London SW1H 9NH.

Pereira, Nancy, and Ernesto Cardoso. *New Gestures, New Gazes.* Rio de Janeiro: Instituto de Estudos da Religiao, 1993.

Poemas, Oraciones & Canciones. Rio de Janeiro: Eggys, 1993.

Songs of Zion. Nashville: Abingdon Press, 1981.

Sound the Bamboo. Manila: Christian Conference of Asia and the Asian Institute for Liturgy and Music, 1990. Inquiries can be addressed to The Asian Institute for Liturgy and Music, P.O. Box 3167, Manila 1099, Philippines.

Thuma Mina: International Ecumenical Hymnbook. Munchen-Berlin: Strube Verlag and Basel: Basileia Verlag, 1995.

Union Hymnal Committee. *Hymns of Universal Praise*. Shanghai: Christian Literature Society for China, 1936.

Wren, Brian. *Visions & Revisions*. Carol Stream, Ill.: Hope Publishing, 1997.

Yang, E. Y. I. *Chinese Christian Hymns by Chinese Writers with Chinese Tunes*. English translations by Frank W. Price. Richmond, Va.: Satterwhite Press, 1953.

Liturgical Resources

Bowyer, O. Richard, Betty L. Hart, and Charlotte A. Meade. *Prayer in the Black Tradition*. Nashville: Upper Room, 1986.

Carden, John, ed. *A Procession of Prayers: Meditations and Prayers from around the World*. Geneva: WCC Publications, 1998.

Cardoso, Ernesto Barros. *Whole Life, Holy Life*. Rio de Janeiro: Instituto de Estudos da Religiao, 1993.

In Spirit and in Truth: A Worship Book. Geneva: World Council of Churches, 1991.

The Iona Community Worship Book. Glasgow: Wild Goose Publications of the Iona Community, 1994.

Morely, Janet. *All Desires Known*. London: SPCK, 1992.

Pereira, Nancy and Ernesto Cardoso. *New Gestures, New Gazes*. Rio de Janeiro: Instituto de Estudos da Religiao, 1993.

Poemas, Oraciones & Canciones. Rio de Janeiro: Eggys, 1993.

Tirabassi, Maren C. and Kathy Wonson Eddy. *Gifts of Many Cultures: Worship Resources for the Global Community*. Cleveland: United Church Press, 1995.

Tutu, Desmond. *An African Prayer Book*. New York: Doubleday, 1995.

Van de Weyer, Robert. *Celtic Prayers*. Nashville: Abingdon Press, 1997.

Appendix B
Hymns from around the World Found in North American Hymnals

Our hymnals are multicultural in many ways representing the various cultures of Europe. Since North American and British hymnody are more familiar to our various congregations, it is not included here. Appendix C will list some of those hymns where new lyrics have been written to traditional hymn tunes. This appendix lists the more recent hymnody from cultures around the world that have become included in the hymnals of mainline Protestant denominations. These hymns can be tremendous resources for multicultural congregations. The hymns are listed in three categories: (1) Liturgical Year, (2) Service Music, and (3) Topical Index. Following the title of a hymn will be a two- or three-letter code (e.g., UMH) and page number representing the following hymnals:

CH   *Chalice Hymnal* (Disciples of Christ). St. Louis: Chalice Press, 1995.

EH   *The Hymnal* (Episcopalian). New York: Church Hymnal Corporation, 1982.

HCW   *Hymnbook for Christian Worship* (American Baptist). St. Louis: Bethany Press, 1970.

LH   *Lutheran Book of Worship and Hymnal.* Minneapolis: Augsburg Press, 1972.

NCH   *New Century Hymnal* (United Church of Christ). Cleveland: Pilgrim Press, 1995.

PH   *The Presbyterian Hymnal.* Louisville, Ky.: Westminster/ John Knox Press, 1990.

UMH   *The United Methodist Hymnal.* Nashville: United Methodist Publishing House, 1989.

VU   *Voices United* (United Church of Canada). Ontario: United Church Publishing House, 1996.

WOV   *With One Voice: A Lutheran Resource for Worship.* Minneapolis: Augsburg Fortress Press, 1995.

Liturgical Year

Advent

HISPANIC HYMNS/SONGS:

"Cold December Flies Away" (*En el Frio Invernal*)   UMH 233
Spain:

"All the Earth Is Waiting" (*Toda la Tierra*)   CH 139, NCH 121,
UMH 210, WOV 629

TAIZÉ COMMUNITY (FRANCE) HYMNS/SONGS:

"Prepare the Way of the Lord"   CH 121, UMH 207

Christmas

AFRICAN HYMNS/SONGS:
Malawi:

"That Boy-Child of Mary"   UMH 241

AFRICAN AMERICAN HYMNS/SONGS/SPIRITUALS:

"Go, Tell It on the Mountain"   CH 167, NCH 154,
UMH 251
"It Was Poor Little Jesus"   EH 468
"Jesus, Jesus, Oh, What a Wonderful Child"   NCH 136
"There's a Star in the East"   WOV 645

ASIAN HYMNS/SONGS:
Japan:

"In a Lowly Manger Born"   NCH 162
"Sheep Fast Asleep" (*Hitsuji wa nemureri*)   NCH 137

Philippines:

"Let Us Even Now Go to Bethlehem"
(*Manglakat na Kita sa Belen*)   NCH 142

HISPANIC HYMNS/SONGS:

"Oh, Sleep Now, Holy Baby" (*Duérmete Niño Lindo*)   EH 113

Argentina:

"Gloria, Gloria, Gloria"   WOV 637

Puerto Rico:

"As Shepherds Filled with Joy" (*Pastores a Belén*)   NCH 149

Venezuela:
| "Child So Lovely" (*Niño Lindo*) | UMH 222 |

NATIVE AMERICAN HYMNS/SONGS:
First Peoples of Canada:
| "'Twas in the Moon of Wintertime" | UMH 244 |

TAIZÉ COMMUNITY (FRANCE) HYMNS/SONGS:
| "Gloria" | WOV 640 |

Epiphany

ASIAN HYMNS/SONGS:
Korea:
| "Lovely Star in the Sky" | CH 175 |

Philippines:
| "Let Us Even Now Go to Bethlehem" | |
| (*Manglakat na Kita sa Belen*) | NCH 142 |

HISPANIC HYMNS/SONGS:
Puerto Rico:
"From a Distant Home"	
(*De Tierra Lejana Venimos*)	UMH 243
"The Magi Who to Bethlehem Did Go"	
(*Los magos que llegaron a Belén*)	NCH 155

Lent

AFRICAN AMERICAN HYMNS/SONGS/SPIRITUALS:
Good Friday
"He Never Said a Mumbalin' Word"	CH 208, UMH 291
"They Crucified My Lord"	VU 141
"Were You There"	CH 198, EH 172,
	HCW 161, NCH 229, PH 102,
	UMH 288, VU 144

ASIAN HYMNS/SONGS:
Japan:
"Ah, What Shame I Have to Bear"	NCH 203
Good Friday	
"Why Has God Forsaken Me"	PH 406

Philippines:
Palm/Passion Sunday
"All Glory, Laud, and Honor"   NCH 217
Holy Thursday
"When Twilight Comes" (*Awit Sa Dapit Hapon*)   PH 537

HISPANIC HYMNS/SONGS:
Mexico:
Palm/Passion Sunday
"Filled with Excitement" (*Mantos y Palmas*)   NCH 214,
                                                 UMH 279

TAIZÉ COMMUNITY (FRANCE) HYMNS/SONGS:
Holy Week
"Stay Here"   WOV 667
Good Friday
"Jesus Remember Me"   CH 569, UMH 488,
                                       VU 148, WOV 740

Easter

AFRICAN AMERICAN HYMNS/SONGS/SPIRITUALS:
"Christ Rose up from the Dead"   NCH 239
"He Rose"   UMH 316

Ascension
"He Is King of Kings"   PH 153

ASIAN HYMNS/SONGS:
Philippines:
"I'll Shout the Name of Christ Who Lives"   NCH 234

AUSTRALIAN HYMNS/SONGS:
Tanzania:
"Christ Has Arisen, Alleluia"   WOV 678

HISPANIC HYMNS/SONGS:
Argentina:
"Christ Is Living" (*Cristo Vive!*)
                                     NCH 235, PH 109,
                                            UMH 313
(also translated "Christ Is Risen" and "Christ Lives")

Spain:
  "Walk on, O People of God"
    (*Camina, Pueblo de Diós*)   NCH 614, PH 296,
                                                             UMH 305
    (also translated "Go Forth, O People of God")

Israeli Hymns/Songs:
  "Christ Is Risen from the Dead"   VU 167

Pentecost

African Hymns/Songs:
Nigeria
  "Come Holy Spirit, Come" (Wa Wa Wa Emimimo)   VU 383,
                                                             WOV 681
Swahili:
  "Gracious Spirit, Heed Our Pleading"   WOV 687

Taizé Community (France) Hymns/Songs:
  "Come, Holy Spirit"   VU 208
  "Holy Spirit, Come to Us" (*Veni Sancte Spiritus*)   WOV 686

Service Music

Gathering

African Hymns/Songs:
Zimbabwe:
  "Come, All You People" (*Uyai mose*)   WOV 717

Asian Hymns/Songs:
China:
  "God Be Praised at Early Morn"
    (*Qing-chen zao qi zan-mei Shen*)   VU 414

Japan:
  "Here, O Lord, Your Servants Gather"   CH 278, PH 465,
                                                             UMH 552

Hispanic Hymns/Songs:
  "O Look and Wonder" (*Miren Que Bueno!*)   CH 292
  "Together" (*Unidos*)   CH 496

Confession/Forgiveness

ASIAN HYMNS/SONGS:

Korea:

"Come Back Quickly to the Lord"	UMH 343
"O Come Unto the Lord"	PH 381

Singapore:

"Lord, Have Mercy"	CH 299

HISPANIC HYMNS/SONGS:

"Have Mercy, Lord, on Me" (*Piedad*)	PH 395, WOV 605
"In the Beginning" (*En el Princípio*)	CH 652

Latin America:

"O God, I Want to Enter" (*Señor, Yo Quiero Entrar*)	CH 291

NATIVE AMERICAN HYMNS/SONGS:

Dakota:

"Hear the Good News of Salvation" (*Wotanin Waste Nahon Po*)	PH 355

TAIZÉ COMMUNITY (FRANCE) HYMNS/SONGS:

"Kyrie Eleison" (Christ Have Mercy)	UMH 484

Prayer

AFRICAN HYMNS/SONGS:

South Africa:

"Send Me, Jesus (Lord)" (*Thuma Mina*)	CH 447, NCH 360, UMH 497, VU 572, WOV 773

AFRICAN AMERICAN HYMNS/SONGS/SPIRITUALS:

"It's Me, It's Me, O Lord"	UMH 352
"Kum Ba Yah"	CH 590
"Not My Brother, Nor My Sister" (Standing in the Need of Prayer)	NCH 519
"Standing in the Need of Prayer"	CH 579

ASIAN HYMNS/SONGS:

Vietnam:

"My Prayer Rises to Heaven"	UMH 498

CARIBBEAN HYMNS/SONGS:
West Indies:
    "The Lord's Prayer"   UMH 271

NATIVE AMERICAN HYMNS/SONGS:
Kiowa:
    "Great Spirit, Now I Pray"
       (*Daw-Kee, Aim Daw-Tsi-Taw*)   UMH 330

TAIZÉ COMMUNITY (FRANCE) HYMNS/SONGS:
    "Give to Us Your Peace"   CH 296
    "O Lord, Hear My Prayer"   WOV 772

God's Word

ASIAN HYMNS/SONGS:
Japan:
    "Make a Gift of Your Holy Word"
       (*Mikotoba o kudasai*)   NCH 317
    "Send Your Word"   UMH 195

AUSTRALIAN HYMNS/SONGS:
Tanzania:
    "Listen, God Is Calling"   WOV 712

ISRAELI HYMNS/SONGS:
    "Open Your Ears, O Faithful People"   EH 536, VU 272,
                                         WOV 715

Texts

ASIAN HYMNS/SONGS:
China:
    "Great Are Your Mercies, O My Maker"
       (Mt. 6:25–34)   PH 352

Indonesia:
    "Ask Your God" (Mt. 7:7)   CH 302

HISPANIC HYMNS/SONGS:
    "Sing, Deborah, Sing" (*Canta, Debora, Canta*)
    (Judges 5)   UMH 81

Latin America:
  "I Want to Be" (*Yo Quiero Ser*) (Isa. 64:8)   CH 520

Israeli Hymns/Songs:
  "Lift Up the Gates Eternal" (Psalm 24)   PH 177

Baptism

African American Hymns/Songs/Spirituals:
  "Take Me to the Water"   CH 367, NCH 322
  "Wade in the Water"   CH 371

Eucharist/Holy Communion

African Hymns/Songs:
South Africa:
  "Hallelujah! We Sing Your Praises"   WOV 722

African American Hymns/Songs/Spirituals:
  "I'm Gonna Eat at the Welcome Table"   CH 424
  "Let Us Break Bread Together"   CH 425, EH 325,
                                          HCW 315, LH 212, NCH 330,
                                          PH 513, UMH 618, VU 480

Asian Hymns/Songs:
China:
  "For the Bread Which You Have Broken"   EH 340
  "O Bread of Life for Sinners Broken"   EH 342, NCH 333
  "The Bread of Life for All Is Broken"   UMH 633

Taiwan:
  "For the Bread Which You Have Broken"   UMH 615

Caribbean Hymns/Songs:
Jamaica:
  "Let Us Talents and Tongues Employ"   CH 422, NCH 347,
                                               PH 514, WOV 754

Hispanic Hymns/Songs:
  "Unto Your Table, Lord" (*Hasta Tu Altar*)   CH 421

Nicaragua:
  "Now We Offer" (*Te Ofrecemos*)   WOV 761

"We Are People on a Journey"
   (*Somos pueblo que camina*)   NCH 340

Spain:
   "Sheaves of Summer" (*Una Espiga*)   CH, 396, NCH 338,
                               PH 518, UMH 637,
                                   WOV 708
   "You Are the Seed" (*Sois la Semilla*)   CH 478, NCH 528,
                               UMH 583, WOV 753

TAIZÉ COMMUNITY (FRANCE) HYMNS/SONGS:
   "Eat This Bread"   CH 414, UMH 628,
                               VU 466, WOV 709

Sending Forth

AFRICAN HYMNS/SONGS:
South Africa:
   "Hallelujah! We Sing Your Praises"   WOV 722

AFRICAN AMERICAN HYMNS/SONGS/SPIRITUALS:
   "God Be with You"   CH 435
   "Lord, Make Us More Holy"   PH 536

ASIAN HYMNS/SONGS:
China:
   "May the Lord, Mighty God"   PH 596

HISPANIC HYMNS/SONGS:
Argentina:
   "May the God of Hope Go with Us"   VU 424
   "Song of Hope" (*Canto de Esperanza*)   PH 432

Spain:
   "Go Forth, O People of God"
      (*Camina, Pueblo de Diós*)   NCH 614, PH 296, UMH 305
   (also translated "Walk On, O People of God")

ISRAELI HYMNS/SONGS:
   "Shalom Chaverim"   CH 438, EH 714, PH 537,
                            UMH 667, WOV 724

Topical Index

Birthday

ASIAN HYMNS/SONGS:

Philippines:

"What a Glad Day"
(*Malipayong Adlaw'ng Natawhan*)   NCH 428

Christian Journey

AFRICAN HYMNS/SONGS:

South Africa:

"We Are Marching in the Light of God"
(*Siyahamba*)   CH 442, NCH 526,
                                 VU 646, WOV 650

AFRICAN AMERICAN HYMNS/SONGS/SPIRITUALS:

"Do Lord, Remember Me"   UMH 527
"Guide My Feet"   NCH 497, PH 354
"We Are Climbing Jacob's Ladder"   NCH 500, UMH 418

Church

AFRICAN AMERICAN HYMNS/SONGS SPIRITUALS:

"Old Ship of Zion"   CH 539, NCH 310, UMH 345

Creation

ASIAN HYMNS/SONGS:

China:

"Golden Breaks the Dawn"   NCH 470

Japan:

"Para, Para, Pitter Pat"   VU 309

Korea:

"God Made All People of the World"   CH 685

Philippines:

"Lord, Your Hands Have Formed"   WOV 727

Taiwan:

"God Created Heaven and Earth" PH 290, UMH 151,
VU 251

HISPANIC HYMNS/SONGS:

"Let's Sing Unto the Lord" (*Cantemos al Señor*) UMH 149,
WOV 726

(also translated "O Sing to God Above")

NATIVE AMERICAN HYMNS/SONGS:
Dakota:

"Many and Great, O God" EH 385, PH 271, UMH 148,
VU 308, WOV 794

Discipleship

AFRICAN HYMNS/SONGS:
South Africa:

"Send Me, Jesus" (*Thuma Mina*) CH 447, NCH 360,
UMH 497, VU 572,
WOV 773

(also translated "Send Me, Lord")

AFRICAN AMERICAN HYMNS/SONGS/SPIRITUALS:

"I'm Gonna Live So God Can Use Me" CH 614, PH 369,
VU 575
"Keep Your Lamps Trimmed and Burning" NCH 369
"Lord, I Want to Be a Christian" CH 589, NCH 454,
PH 372, UMH 402

ASIAN HYMNS/SONGS:
Korea:

"I Will Go Wherever God Calls" CH 474
"Now I Have New Life in Christ" CH 513

Philippines:

"Dear Lord, Lead Me Day by Day" VU 568

HAWAIIAN HYMNS/SONGS:

"Three Greatest Things" (*Ekolu Mea Nui*) NCH 496

HISPANIC HYMNS/SONGS:

Latin America:

"Loving Only You, O Christ"
(*Amarte Solo a Ti, Señor*)   CH 522

Spain:

"Lord, You Have Come to the Lakeshore"
(*Tú Has Venido a la Orilla*)   CH 342, NCH 173,
                    PH 377, UMH 344, WOV 784
"You Are the Seed" (*Sois la Semilla*)   CH 478, NCH 528,
                    UMH 583, WOV 753

Eventide

ASIAN HYMNS/SONGS:

Philippines:

"When Twilight Comes" (*Awit Sa Dapit Hapon*)   PH 537

Exodus

AFRICAN AMERICAN HYMNS/SONGS/SPIRITUALS:

"Go Down, Moses"   CH 663, UMH 448
"O Mary, Don't You Weep"   UMH 134
"When Israel Was in Egypt's Land"   EH 648, NCH 572,
                    PH 334, WOV 670

ISRAELI HYMNS/SONGS:

"If Our God Had Simply Saved Us"   VU 131
"Praise Our Great and Gracious Lord"   EH 393

Faith

AFRICAN AMERICAN HYMNS/SONGS/SPIRITUALS:

"Come Out the Wilderness"   UMH 416
"I Heard My Mother Say"   NCH 409
"I Love the Lord"   CH 598
"I Shall Not Be Moved"   CH 615
"I Will Trust in the Lord"   NCH 416
"I've Got a Feeling"   NCH 458
"Over My Head"   NCH 514
"Somebody's Calling My Name"   PH 382

ASIAN HYMNS/SONGS:

Japan:

"In Lonely Mountain Ways" (*Ya-ma-ji, Ko-e-te*)   VU 666

HISPANIC HYMNS/SONGS:

"I Am Living, Lord, Because You Live"
(*Yo Vivo, Señor, Porque Tú Vives*)   CH 617
"Jesus Christ Is Lord of All" (*Jesucristo es el Señor*)   CH 107

Mexico:

"O Jesus, My King and My Sovereign"
(*Jesús es Mi Rey Soberano*)   CH 109, PH 157,
      UMH 180
"When We Are Living" (*Pues Si Vivimos*)   CH 536, NCH 499,
      PH 400, UMH 356

God's Nature

HISPANIC HYMNS/SONGS:

El Salvador:

"Holy, Holy, Holy" (*Santo, Santo, Santo*)   CH 111, VU 944

ISRAELI HYMNS/SONGS:

"Praise to the Living God"   EH 372, LH 544,
      PH 488, UMH 116
"The God of Abraham Praise"   LH 544

TAIZÉ COMMUNITY (FRANCE) HYMNS/SONGS:

"Nothing Can Trouble (*Nada Te Turbe*)   VU 290

Help in Times of Trial

AFRICAN AMERICAN HYMNS/SONGS/SPIRITUALS:

"I Love You, God, Who Heard My Cry"   NCH 511, PH 362,
      VU 617
"I Want Jesus to Walk with Me"   CH 627, NCH 490,
      PH 363, UMH 521, WOV 660
"I'm So Glad, Jesus Lifted Me"   CH 529, NCH 474,
      WOV 672
"Nobody Knows the Trouble I See"   UMH 520
"Precious Lord, Take My Hand"   CH 628, PH 404,
      UMH 474, VU 670, WOV 731
"The Lord Will Make a Way Somehow"   CH 620
"There Is a Balm in Gilead"   CH 501, EH 676, PH 394,
      UMH 375, VU 612, WOV 737

ASIAN HYMNS/SONGS:

"Though Falsely Some Revile or Hate Me"   NCH 477

Korea:

"Lonely the Boat"
(*Kahm Kahm Hahn Bom Sanaoon*)   PH 373, UMH 476

Laos/Thailand:
"Come, All of You"   UMH 350

HUNGARIAN HYMNS/SONGS:
"Lift Up Your Head, O Martyrs, Weeping"   NCH 445

PAKISTANI/NORTH INDIAN HYMNS/SONGS:
"Refuge" (*Saranam, Saranam*)   UMH 523

Holy Spirit

AFRICAN HYMNS/SONGS:
Nigeria:

"Come, Holy Spirit, Come" (*Wa wa wa Emimimo*)   VU 383,
                                                  WOV 681
"Every Time I Feel the Spirit"   CH 592, NCH 282,
                                         PH 315, UMH 404
"I'm Goin' a Sing When the Spirit Says Sing"   UMH 333

Jesus' Life and Ministry

AFRICAN HYMNS/SONGS:
Ghana:
"Christ the Worker"   EH 611

AFRICAN AMERICAN HYMNS/SONGS/SPIRITUALS:
"Amen, Amen"   NCH 161, PH 299
"In the Morning When I Rise"   WOV 777

ASIAN HYMNS/SONGS:
Japan:
"In Old Galilee, When Sweet Breezes Blew"
(*Gariraya no kaze kaoru oka de*)   VU 354

Korea:
"Christ, You Are the Fullness"   PH 346

Last Times

AFRICAN AMERICAN HYMNS/SONGS/SPIRITUALS:

"Fix Me, Jesus"	UMH 655
"Great Day"	PH 445
"Hush, Hush, Somebody's Calling My Name"	NCH 604
"I Want to Be Ready"	NCH 616, UMH 722
"My Lord What a Morning"	CH 708, PH 449, UMH 719, VU 708, WOV 627
"Nobody Knows the Trouble I See"	UMH 520
"O Mary, Don't You Weep"	UMH 134
"Precious Lord, Take My Hand"	CH 628, PH 404, UMH 474, VU 670, WOV 731
"Steal Away to Jesus"	CH 644, NCH 599, UMH 704
"Swing Low, Sweet Chariot"	CH 643, UMH 703

Love

AFRICAN AMERICAN HYMNS/SONGS/SPIRITUALS:

"I've Just Come from the Fountain"	WOV 696
"Woke Up This Morning"	CH 623

ASIAN HYMNS/SONGS:

Korea:

"The Savior's Wondrous Love"	HCW 267
"With the Wings of Our Mind"	CH 667

HISPANIC HYMNS/SONGS:

Puerto Rico:

"A New Commandment" (*Un mandamiento Nuevo*)	NCH 389
"United by God's Love" (*En Santa Hermandad*)	NCH 392

TAIZÉ HYMNS/SONGS:

"Live in Charity"	CH 523
"Where True Love and Charity" (*Ubi Caritas et Amor*)	WOV 665

Peace and Justice

AFRICAN HYMNS/SONGS:

South Africa:

"We Shall Not Give Up the Fight"	NCH 437

AFRICAN AMERICAN HYMNS/SONGS/SPIRITUALS:

"Children of God"	NCH 533
"Down by the Riverside"	CH 673
"We Shall Overcome"	CH 630, UMH 533

ASIAN HYMNS/SONGS:

Korea:

"I Will Go Wherever God Calls"	CH 474
"With the Wings of Our Mind" (*Ttugain Maum*)	CH 667, VU 698

Laos/Thailand:

"Come, All of You"	UMH 350

Philippines:

"Enter in the Realm of God (lyrics by Lavon Bayler)	NCH 615

HAWAIIAN HYMNS/SONGS:

"The Queen's Prayer" (*O Kou Aloha No*)	NCH 580

HISPANIC HYMNS/SONGS:

"In the Beginning" (*En el Princípio*)	CH 652
"Together" (*Unidos*)	CH 496
"When a Poor One" (*Cuando el Pobre*)	CH 662, PH 407, UMH 434, VU 702

Mexico:

"You Shall Prophesy, All My People" (*Profetiza, Pueblo Mía*)	NCH 578

Nicaragua:

"We Are People on a Journey" (*Somos Pueblo que Camina*)	NCH 340

El Salvador:

"Holy, Holy, Holy" (*Santo, Santo, Santo*)	CH 111, VU 944

Spain:

"Hear the Voice of God, So Tender" (lyrics by Lavon Bayler)	NCH 174

ISRAELI HYMNS/SONGS:
"Community of Christ"
(lyrics by Shirley Erena Murray)   NCH 314

Praise
AFRICAN HYMNS/SONGS:
Cameroon:
"Let Us Praise the God of Truth"   VU 237

South Africa:
"Alleluia"   WOV 610
"Amen, We Praise Your Name"
(*Amen, Siakudumisa*)   WOV 768
"Hosanna" (*Sanna, Sannanina*)   VU 128
"Sing Amen" (*Asithi: Amen*)   VU 431

AFRICAN AMERICAN HYMNS/SONGS/SPIRITUALS:
"Thank You, Lord"   CH 531

ASIAN HYMNS/SONGS:
China:
"God be Praised at Early Morn"
(*Qing-chen zao qi zan-mei Shen*)   VU 414

Japan:
"Praise to God"   VU 243

Java:
"Amen, Hallelujah"   WOV 792

Philippines:
"Dear Lord, Lead Me Day by Day"   UMH 411, VU 568
"Sing with Hearts"   PH 484

CARIBBEAN HYMNS/SONGS:
West Indies:
"Halle, Halle, Hallelujah"   NCH 236, WOV 612

HISPANIC HYMNS/SONGS:
Brazil:
"O Sing to the Lord" (*Cantad al Señor*)   PH 472, VU 241,
                                                WOV 795

Peru:

   "Glory to God, Glory in the Highest"   WOV 788

ISRAELI HYMNS/SONGS:

   "Praise Our Great and Gracious Lord"   EH 393
   "The Living God Be Praised"   VU 255

NATIVE AMERICAN HYMNS/SONGS:

Muscogee:

   "Hallelujah" (*Heleluyan*)   PH 595, UMH 78, WOV 609

PAKISTANI/NORTH INDIAN HYMNS/SONGS:

   "Jaya Ho" (Victory Hymn)   UMH 478, VU 252

Servanthood

AFRICAN HYMNS/SONGS:

   "Jesu, Jesu, Fill Us with Your Love"   EH 602, NCH 498,
                                      PH 367, UMH 432,
                                      VU 593, WOV 785

ASIAN HYMNS/SONGS:

China:

   "In All the Seasons Seeking God"   CH 607
   "Rise to Greet the Sun"   UMH 678

Thanksgiving/Harvest

ASIAN HYMNS/SONGS:

China:

   "Praise Our God Above"   NCH 424, PH 480

HISPANIC HYMNS/SONGS:

Latin America:

   "O What Shall I Render?" (*Con Que Pagaremos?*)   PH 557

Trinity

ASIAN HYMNS/SONGS:

Philippines:

   "O God in Heaven"   NCH 279, UMH 119

CARIBBEAN HYMNS/SONGS:
West Indies:
    "Come, Be Glad!"   CH 329

Unity in Diversity

AFRICAN AMERICAN HYMNS/SONGS/SPIRITUALS:
    "In Christ There Is No East or West"   EH 529, HCW 269,
        NCH 394, PH 440,
        UMH 548, VU 606

ASIAN HYMNS/SONGS:
Japan:
    "Here, O Lord, Your Servants Gather"   CH 278, UMH 552

HISPANIC HYMNS/SONGS:
Latin America:
    "We're United in Jesus" (*Somos Uno en Cristo*)   CH 493

Mexico:
    "Sing of Colors" (*De Colores*)   NCH 402

Witness

AFRICAN AMERICAN HYMNS/SONGS/SPIRITUALS:
    "I've Got Peace Like a River"   CH 530, NCH 478,
        PH 368, VU 577
    "This Little Light of Mine"   NCH 525, UMH 585
    "This Little Light/This Joy I Have"   NCH 524

Appendix C
Traditional Hymn Tunes
with New Lyrics

Many American and British hymn writers are creating new lyrics to be sung to traditional hymn tunes. Hymns of this type keep people rooted in the familiar tunes that missionaries transported around the world while providing more contemporary images for multicultural congregations. Below is a list of many of these hymns that can be found in mainline Protestant hymnals. The hymns are organized around three categories: (1) Liturgical Year, (2) Service Music, and (3) Topical Index. Following each hymn title is a two- or three-letter code (e.g., NCH) and page number representing one of these hymnals:

CH   *Chalice Hymnal* (Disciples of Christ). St. Louis: Chalice Press, 1995.

EH   *The Hymnal* (Episcopalian). New York: Church Hymnal Corporation, 1982.

LH   *Lutheran Book of Worship and Hymnal.* Minneapolis: Augsburg Press, 1972.

NCH   *New Century Hymnal* (United Church of Christ). Cleveland: Pilgrim Press, 1995.

PH   *The Presbyterian Hymnal.* Louisville, Ky.: Westminster/ John Knox Press, 1990.

UMH   The United Methodist Hymnal. Nashville: United Methodist Publishing House, 1989.

VU   *Voices United* (United Church of Canada). Ontario: United Church Publishing House, 1996.

WOV   *With One Voice: A Lutheran Resource for Worship.* Minneapolis: Augsburg Fortress Press, 1995.

Liturgical Year

(and American cultural holidays)

Advent

"My Heart Sings Out with Joyful Praise"	NCH 106
"My Soul Gives Glory to My God"	CH 130, NCH 119, UMH 198
"Now Bless the God of Israel"	NCH 110
"One Candle Is Lit"	CH 128

Epiphany

"Brightest and Best"	CH 174

Lent

"To Mock Your Reign, O Dearest Lord"	UMH 285
"Who Would Have Believed It?"	CH 213

Holy Thursday

"An Upper Room Did Our Lord Prepare"	CH 385, PH 94
"Great God! Your Love Has Called Us"	PH 353, UMH 579, WOV 653

Easter

"Christ Is Alive! Let Christians Sing"	EH 182, LH 363, PH 108, UMH 318
"Christ Is Risen! Shout Hosanna"	CH 222, PH 104, UMH 307, WOV 672

Pentecost

"Let Every Christian Pray"	NCH 261, PH 130
"On Pentecost They Gathered"	CH 237, NCH 272, PH 128

Independence Day

"How Beautiful, Our Spacious Skies"	NCH 594

All Saints Day

"God, We Thank You for Our People"	NCH 376
"Rejoice in God's Saints"	CH 476, UMH 708, WOV 689

Thanksgiving/Harvest

"Come Sing a Song of Harvest"	CH 719, PH 558, NCH 140
"For the Fruit of All Creation"	CH 714, NCH 425, WOV 760

Service Music

Gathering

"God, Whose Love Is Reigning o'er Us"	UMH 100
"Loving Lord, as Now We Gather"	CH 427
"O God of Vision"	CH 288
"Praise with Joy the World's Creator"	NCH 273
"Womb of Life, and Source of Being"	CH 14, NCH 274

Confession/Forgiveness

"God! When Human Bonds Are Broken"	WOV 735
"Great God, Your Love Has Called Us"	PH 353, UMH 579, WOV 666

Prayer

"In Solitude"	NCH 521

Texts

"The Lord's My Shepherd" (Ps. 23)	PH 274

Offering

"Accept, O God, the Gifts We Bring"	CH 379

Baptism

"Lord, When You Came to Jordan"	CH 177, PH 71
"Wash, O God, Our Sons and Daughters"	CH 365, UMH 605
"When Jesus Came to Jordan"	UMH 252, WOV 647
"With Grateful Hearts Our Faith Confessing"	PH 497
"Wonder of Wonders, Here Revealed"	CH 378, PH 499, NCH 328

Eucharist/Communion

Wedding

Topical Index

Christian Journey

Creation

Discipleship

"Jesus Christ Is Waiting"	VU 117
"We Are Living, We Are Dwelling"	CH 472
"Will You Come and Follow Me"	VU 567
"Whom Shall I Send?"	UMH 582

Exodus

"Lead On, O Cloud of Presence"	CH 633

Faith

"God (Lord), When I Came into This Life"	NCH 354, PH 522
"When Our Confidence Is Shaken"	CH 534, UMH 505

God's Nature

"God Reigns o'er All the Earth"	NCH 21
"God, Whose Love Is Reigning o'er Us"	UMH 100
"How Can We Name a Love"	UMH 111

Help in Times of Trial

"O Savior, in This Quiet Place"	PH 390

Holy Spirit

"Of All the Spirit's Gifts to Me"	UMH 336

Jesus' Life and Ministry

"Down to Earth, as a Dove"	PH 300
"O Christ, the Healer"	CH 503, NCH 175, PH 380, UMH 265

Last Things

"How Blest Are They Who Trust in Christ"	CH 646, NCH 365
"Let Hope and Sorrow Now Unite"	CH 639
"Lord of the Living"	PH 529

Love

"Great God, Your Love Has Called Us"	PH 353,
	UMH 579, WOV 666
"Of All the Spirit's Gifts to Me"	UMH 336

Peace and Justice

"Alleluia! Hear God's Story"	CH 330
"Arise, Your Light Is Come"	NCH 164,
	PH 411, WOV 652
"Called as Partners in Christ's Service"	CH 453
"Creating God, Your Fingers Trace"	CH 335,
	UMH 109, WOV 757
"Diverse in Culture, Nation, Race"	CH 485
"For the Healing of the Nations"	NCH 576, UMH 428
"Jesus Christ Is Waiting"	VU 117
"Lead On, O Cloud of Presence"	CH 633
"Let Justice Flow like Streams"	NCH 588, WOV 763
"Live into Hope"	PH 332
"O For a World"	CH 683, NCH 575
"O God of Earth and Altar"	CH 724, PH 291,
	NCH 582
"O God of Earth and Space"	PH 274
"The Church of Christ in Every Age"	CH 475, NCH 306,
	PH 421
"We Cannot Own the Sunlit Sky"	CH 684, NCH 563
"We Utter Our Cry"	UMH 439
"When, in Awe of God's Creation"	CH 688
"Why Stand So Far Away, My God?"	CH 671

Praise

"To God Compose a Song of Joy"	NCH 36

Prayer

"O Christ, the Healer"	CH 503, PH 380,
	NCH 175, UMH 265
"O Savior, in This Quiet Place"	PH 390
"Why Stand So Far Away, My God?"	CH 671

Thanksgiving
"God, We Thank You for Our People"   NCH 376

Trinity
"Praise with Joy the World's Creator"   NCH 273
"Womb of Life, and Source of Being"   CH 14, NCH 274

Unity in Diversity
"Diverse in Culture, Nation, Race"   CH 485
"How Beautiful, Our Spacious Skies"   NCH 594

Witness
"God, You Spin the Whirling Planets"   PH 285
"There's a Spirit in the Air"   CH 257, NCH 294,
                                                     UMH 192
"We Meet You, O Christ"   PH 311
"Your Ways Are Not Our Own"   NCH 170

Appendix D
Questionnaire

(This questionnaire was designed by Rev. Ben Ellis, pastor of a multicultural congregation in Rialto, California.)

Name _____

Address _____

_____

Phone _____

Native Culture _____

Years in U.S. _____

Denominations _____

In this questionnaire I use the words "Home Church" or "Home Culture" for those in which we were born and grew. These are in quotes in recognition that this place and church are your new home.

BASICS:

1. Is worship in your "home church" more:
   ❏ formal or ❏ informal?

2. Is worship there more:
   ❏ full of energy or ❏ quiet and sacred?

3. What is more important in the churches there:
   ❏ that worship start and end on time, or
   ❏ that all the time that is needed is dedicated to worship.

4. In your "home country" is worship more:
   ❏ free flowing or ❏ structured?

5. Is worship in your "home country"
   ❏ something we do for God, or
   ❏ something God does for us?

6. Thinking about worship in your "home country," rank these in order of importance:
   __ Worship is praise and honor of God.
   __ Worship is a time to introduce Christ to those who have not made a commitment.
   __ Worship is a time when we can grow closer to God and Christ.
   __ Worship is a gathering of the faithful, where we are strengthened to do God's will and mission.

DETAILS ABOUT "HOME CHURCHES":

1. Are children and youth expected to be in worship or out of worship?

   _____

   _____

2. What types of music are used?

   _____

   _____

What instruments?

_____

_____

3. Are bulletins used? If not, how do people know the order of worship?

_____

_____

4. Do laypersons speak or take part in the leading of worship? If so, in what way?

_____

_____

5. What are the different types of prayer used in worship?

_____

_____

6. Do people hug before or after or during worship, or touch in any other way?

_____

_____

7. What symbols are important in your "home church"?

_____

Are these some we could use in our church? Are there things about which we need to be careful?

_____

_____

8. Are banners used? Are other types of art used?

_____

_____

9. Is dance ever used in the churches of your "home country"?

    _____

    _____

10. Is there a meal after worship where all are invited?
    ❏ Always ❏ Once or twice a month
    ❏ Holidays only ❏ Never

11. What important religious events or holidays are celebrated in your "home church"?

    _____

    _____

12. What important holidays are a part of your "home country" each year?

    _____

    _____

13. How are these events celebrated?
    Baptisms: _____

    _____

    Rites of Passage: _____

    _____

    Weddings: _____

    _____

    Funerals: _____

    _____

14. How is holy communion shared?

    _____

    _____

WORKING TOWARD SOLIDARITY:

1. What are the surface differences between your "home culture" and this one?

2. What are important differences between your "home country" and this new home?

3. What are the theological differences between your "home church" and your church here in the United States?

4. What was the pastor's role in your "home church"?

5. How could our church help you grow into a deeper relationship with Christ?

6. How can we retell the stories of your homeland as we take time to share?

NOTES: